APPROACHING DISAPPEARANCE

Copyright © 2013 by Anne McConnell
Chapter IV appeared in different form as "Conversing with a Bavard" in *French Forum* 33.1-2 (2008).

First edition, 2013
All rights reserved

A catalog record for this book is available from the Library of Congress.
ISBN 978-1-56478-808-5

Partially funded by a grant from West Virginia State University, as well as the Illinois Arts Council, a state agency.

www.dalkeyarchive.com

Cover: design and composition by Mikhail Iliatov

Printed on permanent/durable acid-free paper and bound in the United States of America

APPROACHING DISAPPEARANCE

Anne McConnell

DALKEY ARCHIVE PRESS
CHAMPAIGN / LONDON / DUBLIN

Contents

Preface		vii
1.	Approaching Disappearance	17
2.	Franz Kafka and the Disappearance of the Writer	50
3.	Lost in the Labyrinth: Jorge Luis Borges's "The Garden of Forking Paths"	84
4.	The Disappearing Act of Louis-René des Forêts's Bavard	116
5.	Anonymity and the Neutral in Nathalie Sarraute's Tropisms	145
6.	Into the Night: Blanchot's L'arrêt de mort	173
Notes		207
Bibliography		220

Preface

Roland Barthes famously pronounced the "death of the author" in a 1967 essay where he discussed the way that writing necessarily causes the voice to disperse and to lose its origin.[1] No longer could we think of an Author-Creator who serves as the origin of the text, its foundation, the determiner of its meaning. Of course, for Barthes, a recognition of the multiplicity and indeterminacy that arises in writing fundamentally changes the way we approach it; rather than attempting to limit a text to a single, authoritative origin, we might give ourselves over to the rich, endlessly-shifting plurality that writing offers. I mention Barthes as a means of introducing the notion of disappearance that drives my book. While my book focuses on Maurice Blanchot, one of the most significant French writers of the twentieth-century, Barthes's discussion of the author's death resembles the less concrete idea of disappearance that weaves through many of Blanchot's critical works—namely, his 1955 book, *The Space of Literature*. Like we see in Barthes's essay, the concept of an empowered author has no place in Blanchot's work; on the contrary, for Blanchot, the writer necessarily disappears in the process of writing, as he or she no longer has the power to say "I," to create, to make a work come into being. The writer begins writing at the point where he or she can't possibly write, where he or she disappears into an anonymous, passive space in which nothing can be done. That irresolvable paradox remains central to Blanchot's thought, even if we might have difficulty pinning it down in any way. Blanchot's own multiple, dispersed voice in his critical writings and his fictions provides various paths where we might trace the movement of disappearance involved in the work of literature—perhaps beginning with the writer, but also extending to the reader and to the text itself. In the first chapter of this book, I will explore the various ways that the theme of disappearance arises in Blanchot's critical work, focusing on *The Space of Literature* in particular. In the subsequent chapters, I will provide a reading of five short fictions that reflect Blanchot's notion of disappearance from distinct perspectives.

Franz Kafka serves as one of the central figures in *The Space of Literature*, as Blanchot finds in his life and work the struggle of solitude. By solitude, Blanchot does not mean a writer's empowered decision to seclude himself or herself from the world in favor of the literary work; rather, the "essential solitude" characterizes the writer's disappearance, or loss of self, into the impersonal space of the work. In *The Space of Literature*, Blanchot spends much more time grappling with Kafka's *Diaries* than he does with any particular story or novel. Kafka's *Diaries* allow Blanchot to explore the experience of writing as it is documented throughout Kafka's journaling—both in the sense that the *Diaries* include fragments of stories and show us something of the writing process, and in the sense that they demonstrate Kafka's inability to find a place in the world or in his work. After a discussion of Kafka's diaries, and Blanchot's musings upon the diaries, I will dedicate the rest of the chapter to Kafka's narrative, "The Burrow," as it tells not only a story of endless wandering, but also one of profound solitude and disappearance. "The Burrow" takes the reader into the pitch black, underground space where the narrator confronts not only his torturous isolation, but also the threat that he will lose himself to whatever lurks outside, on the other side of the darkness where he is sequestered. Interestingly, the first-person narrative emerges as a sort of journaling, as we read a carefully-documented account of the narrator's construction of his burrow. The narrator's experience, in all its darkness, paradoxically sheds light upon the risk of disappearance that he confronts, as one who responds to the demand of the work.

After considering the notion of solitude in the chapter on "The Burrow," I will look to Jorge Luis Borges's "The Garden of Forking Paths" in order to discuss the question of infinitude as it relates to the disappearance of the literary work beyond the structures seemingly guaranteed by the material book. Borges's story plays with and challenges the possibility of structural containment, allowing the various levels and meanings of his narrative to permeate one another. Within the story, he proposes the idea of an infinite text, and the reader experiences the implications of such an idea when trying to comprehend and interpret that which always escapes beyond the limits of one's grasp. Borges's text purposefully eludes our efforts to limit it, and thus to understand it, which draws our attention to the way the text recedes beyond our vision. In the beginning of my chapter on "The Garden of Forking Paths," I examine the various images of infinitude and labyrinthine space in Borges's work, as a way to approach the notion that any attempt to represent infinitude necessarily dissolves the very thing that one attempts to bring to light. Blanchot in particular takes interest in Borges's figure of "the aleph," an impossible point in space that contains *all* space. Such figures adumbrate Borges's literary universe and take special shape in "The Garden of Forking Paths." As I develop an analysis of this story, I draw particular attention to the way that Borges plays with textual structures, intricately forming them at the same time that he continually suggests the presence of that which infinitely escapes them.

Next, an analysis of des Forêts's narrative *The Bavard* will demonstrate and develop the way that language opens a space for its own disappearance. Des Forêts's narrator invites us to engage with a sort of language that fills and constitutes textual space, despite its utter emptiness. The *bavard*—or "non-stop talker"—says nothing (over a span of roughly one hundred pages), dedicating his narrative only to its own perpetuation and sacrificing its possibility for constructive meaning by revealing it as a simple indulgence, a ruse. In this way, what we have read seems to disappear before us, but we are forced to ponder what remains when nothing is left. The *bavard*'s narrative functions as a sort of game, or magic trick; he actually compares himself to an illusionist, making something appear only to destroy it once we have fallen for the allure of the illusion. While the narrator identifies himself from the very beginning of the text as a *bavard*, and proceeds to tell us precisely about his uncontrollable illness of *bavardage*, the reader nevertheless becomes engaged as the seemingly privileged listener of the confessional-style narrative. We likely recognize the verbosity of narrative, at the same time that we fall into the trap of assigning it meaning—despite what we have been told. As Blanchot explains in *The Space of Literature*, the reader approaches the book as a stone, behind which lies the dead Lazarus; and we can't help but to call him forward, to bring death and absence into the light of day. Des Forêts's narrator plays with this readerly instinct, indulging it before ultimately making himself and his narrative disappear.

One could argue that Sarraute's *Tropisms* seems to begin with the "nothing" that paradoxically emerges at the end of des Forêts's text—at least in the sense that *Tropisms* refuses to identify any single person or thing in a distinct way. The reader never has the illusion of clarity, continuity, or an accessible narrative voice, but rather immediately confronts the remarkable obscurity of the narrative. Sarraute's text abandons the "I" from the beginning, as well as recognizable or discernible characters, locations, or plots. In this way, "he," "she," "it," "here," "there," and so on, disappear into a striking anonymity. This° name-less, place-less space evokes Blanchot's discussion of the neutral—a space, a mode, a voice founded upon no one, nowhere. If Kafka's narratives and his journals explore the struggle of the writer who experiences his disappearance and powerlessness to constitute himself through language, Sarraute's *Tropisms* explores the space of this disappearance, powerlessness, and withdrawn language—"a language which no one speaks."[2] The floating, neutral character of the language, which seems to arise from no one, speaks in the blanks of the text as much as it does throughout the nearly indistinguishable, chapter-like fragments. As we move from fragment to fragment, we seem to have new characters and situations (though characters are only identified as "he," "she," and "they"), rather than a running narrative; at the same time, the fragments bear repetitions and resemblances that make them blur into one another. In Sarraute's text, many of the aspects of more traditional literature that allow us to ground the narrative and characters in something seemingly solid and reassuring have disappeared, leaving us to deal with the irreducible obscurity of the language.

In the final chapter of my book I will turn back to Blanchot, but this time through a narrative text, *L'arrêt de mort*. This *récit* approaches disappearance in a variety of ways, but I focus on the issues of circularity and repetition in particular. As his discussion of the *récit* in *The Book to Come* would indicate, Blanchot's narrative proposes a sort of time outside of time—one that challenges notions of linearity and historicity and that functions by way of repetition and circular paradoxes. Like the work of Orpheus (a central figure in Blanchot's essays), the narrative of *L'arrêt de mort* is founded upon, moves toward, and arises out of its disappearance and impossibility. Michel Foucault writes in "Maurice Blanchot: The Thought From Outside" that *L'arrêt de mort* is "dedicated to the gaze of Orpheus: the gaze that at the wavering threshold of death goes in search of the submerged presence and tries to bring its image back to the light of day."[3] The anonymous narrator of *L'arrêt de mort* retrieves the main character, J., from death, only to lose her again at his own hand when he injects a lethal dose of morphine into her veins. And supposing the narrator remains the same in the two fragments that constitute *L'arrêt de mort*, his transgressive gaze re-emerges when he calls forth a second female character from a deathly state. Aside from those two principal encounters, certain strange, nocturnal scenes repeat themselves throughout the text—such as the spontaneous and confused entry of one of the several female characters, or the narrator himself, into a stranger's room in the middle of the night. No event appears to be singular in this *récit*, but rather finds itself repeated in various ways, as if each penetration of the night forcefully reopens a profound wound that is always, ceaselessly open. In Foucault's brief reference to *L'arrêt de mort*, he seems to touch upon that very idea when he suggests that the narrator's gaze upon J.'s death "is what makes a second woman appear in the middle of the night in an already captive state of stupefaction" (44). Just as Orpheus must have already gazed towards Eurydice in order to initiate his descent to her, each confrontation that the narrator has with the night in *L'arrêt de mort* allows for the one that follows it, and the one that precedes it. Despite the narrator's efforts to ground his experiences in specific dates, times, and historic events, the *récit* exhibits the infinite circularity of Orpheus's descent, which assures his own disappearance, as well as that of Eurydice.

Lastly, I would like to address the fact that I have chosen to work exclusively with short fictions—though the distinction of "short" hardly provides clear parameters by which we might measure a text. As noted above, Blanchot uses the term *récit* when discussing a particular kind of shorter text which he differentiates from the novel. He writes:

> If for the sake of convenience—because this statement cannot be exact—we say that what makes the novel move forward is everyday, collective or personal time, or more precisely, the desire to urge time to speak, then the tale moves forward through that *other* time, it makes that other voyage, which is the passage from the real song to the imaginary song.[4]

Thus, the distinction of the *récit* and the novel, at least according to Blanchot, only indirectly involves the issue of length. If the *récit* is commonly shorter than the novel, this results from the way that the *récit* confines itself to the moment when time becomes the *other* time—a time outside of "everyday, collective or personal time." Blanchot identifies the *récit* as the gulf that inhabits any narrative—an infinite distance that separates the *récit* from its destination, which is also, paradoxically, its origin. While the epic or the novel might contain this bottomless pocket, each also provides the superfluous, excessive, distracted narrative that surrounds it. Blanchot does not critique this; furthermore, he notes that the aimless digressions of the novel paradoxically fulfill the demand of the *récit*. One cannot approach the *récit* with purpose or intent; it exceeds any sense of effort, or mastery. Yet, unlike the novel, the *récit* takes focus, sending any narrative excess to the outside, if only in order to present its own measureless excess. One might therefore conclude that the *récit* takes on a shortened, condensed form as a means of bringing an undistracted attention to its infinite excessiveness.

In *Small Worlds*, a study of minimalism in French literature, Warren Motte suggests the difficulty in identifying something as "small." He writes:

> We designate things as "small" capriciously and according to different registers of perception. We may focus on a thing's physical size; on its duration, intensity, or range; on its import, its significance; on the quantity of the elements composing it; or on the simplicity of its structure. What seems common to all of those interpretive moves is the notion of *reduction* in relation to some more or less explicit norm. Art that insists upon that reduction and mobilizes it as a constructive principle can be termed minimalist.[5] (1, emphasis in original)

In the case of short fiction, or the *récit* if we specifically engage Blanchot's term, smallness, or shortness, indeed assumes a sense of reduction. And as Blanchot suggests, a certain relativity is implied; in other words, "short" fiction is short in relation to the traditional novel. Of course, Blanchot's definition of the *récit* does not necessarily apply to Jorge Luis Borges's short stories, or to Franz Kafka's parables; yet each writer works with a form that plays on the notion of shortness. Borges writes in his "Autobiographical Essay," "The feeling that the great novels *Don Quixote* and *Huckleberry Finn* are virtually shapeless served to reinforce my taste for the short-story form, whose indispensable elements are economy and a clearly stated beginning, middle, and end."[6] Although we might assume a degree of irony in Borges's comment, he clearly celebrates the straightforwardness and the structure of the shortened form. It comes in a neat, organized package that appears to get right to the point. Of course, with Borges and with Blanchot, the ideal of approaching some sort of textual essence does not suggest the pretension of doing so successfully. Rather, as we will see in all of the chapters to come, many short fictions self-consciously play upon their own minimal structures and undermine the notion of shedding excess. In the case of Blanchot's discussion of the *récit*, it would seem that focusing the text on the essential moment of the *récit* simply opens the text up to an illimitable, immeasurable excess. Throughout the book, I will regularly come back to the way the five short texts I have chosen reflect upon "beginning, middle, and end," playing upon their own structures and limits.

I would like to thank West Virginia State University for its generous support of this project. I would also like to express gratitude for my colleagues and academic mentors over the past several years—specifically Professors Warren Motte and Elisabeth Arnould-Bloomfield at the University of Colorado at Boulder.

Chapter 1: Approaching Disappearance

In an essay in *The Book to Come*, Blanchot writes, "literature is going towards itself, towards its essence, which is disappearance."[7] The rest of the essay develops what he means by this statement, building upon Hegel's famous assertion that art is "a thing of the past." Interestingly, Blanchot does not disagree with Hegel on this point, but he comes to vastly different conclusions about what the *end of art* would suggest about the status of art and literature beyond this terminus. Hegel dismisses art from the realm of history and truth, which, from his perspective, pronounces its end.[8] Blanchot, on the other hand, sees this end as a sort of beginning—one which does not have the power to begin or the power to end, but which slips into the movement of its own disappearance. He writes, "Only the work matters, but finally the work is there only to lead to the quest for the work; the work is the impulse that carries us toward the pure point of inspiration from which it comes and which it seems it can reach only by disappearing" (200). Not only does Blanchot's argument demonstrate his characteristically atemporal and circular notion of the approach to the work (the work has its origin at the point it aspires to reach), but it also reveals an important paradox that travels the length of his discussion of writing, reading, and the literary work in *The Space of Literature*. In order for the work to *come forward* in some sense, it must be allowed to disappear—toward itself, its "essence." For Blanchot, this disappearance depends upon a radical reversal where ends open onto an excessive remainder which eludes our power to negate, and therefore necessarily eludes our ability to grasp, perceive, complete, or make appear. With this idea in mind, we can turn to *The Space of Literature* and trace the process of disappearance, as it relates to the writer, the reader, and the work.

Before looking at the first section of *The Space of Literature*, I would like to begin with one of the appendices to this section, "The Essential Solitude and the Solitude of the World." Blanchot reflects upon the separation of "myself from being," as "I" function within the world, negating being in order to make the world appear to me, to my understanding. He explains, "What makes me me is this decision to be by being separate from being—to be *without* being, to be that which owes nothing to being, whose power comes from the refusal to be" (*SL* 251). Following Hegelian logic, Blanchot asserts that the power to negate constitutes man's accomplishment and activity in the world, but he brings attention to the lack of being and to the question of what remains when being lacks.[9] In other words, Blanchot wonders if this activity of negating the world, of refusing being, does not encounter, at the limit of its power, an essential inability to make nothing of the lack of being. He asks, "When being lacks, does this mean that this lack owes nothing to being? Or rather does it mean perhaps that the lack is the being that lies deep in the absence of being—that the lack is what still remains of being when there is nothing?" (253). Blanchot brings us to the question of disappearance here, in the sense that disappearance indicates the process of becoming nothing. And, further, disappearance places emphasis on the inability to *see*, on the recession of the world from our vision, beyond the power to bring it to light. Disappearance, like negation, can be understood in terms of man's power—as giving rise to the appearance of something that would be available to comprehension—but, again, Blanchot's interest concerns the remaining trace of disappearance itself, when the power to make disappear has been exhausted:

> When beings lack, being appears as the depth of the concealment in which it becomes lack. When concealment appears, concealment, having become appearance, makes "everything disappear," but of this "everything has disappeared," it makes another appearance. It makes appearance from then on stem from "everything has disappeared." "Everything has disappeared" appears. This is exactly what we call an *apparition*. It is the "everything has disappeared" appearing in its turn. (253)

For Blanchot, the apparition, the appearance of "everything has disappeared," characterizes the literary work (though the work exceeds categorization in its very disappearance).[10] Writers and readers are pulled into a space in their approach to the work that can only be affirmed in the depth of its concealment. In *The Space of Literature*, Blanchot explores this approach and examines the risk of disappearance involved for those who experience the inability and anonymity of the work's invisible space.

When Blanchot discusses the "essential solitude" in the first section of *The Space of Literature*, he clarifies that this solitude does not result from a writer's empowered choice to sequester him or herself from the world in favor of the work. Blanchot explains, "He who writes the work is set aside; he who has written it is dismissed. He who is dismissed, moreover, doesn't know it. This ignorance preserves him. It distracts him by authorizing him to persevere" (21). There seems to be something about the work that resists, or even prevents, relation, even if the writer depends upon a relation with the work to write. The writer perseveres because the work is never finished, and it is never finished, first of all, because one cannot determine or define any criteria that would make it so. And the work thus draws the writer into an infinite process at the same time that it dismisses his or her participation in the process. The writer gives him or herself over to the work, but the work always recedes beyond the "giving over," which affirms its essential solitude, and the writer's. Blanchot writes, "He whose life depends on the work, either because he is a writer or because he is a reader, belongs to the solitude of that which expresses nothing except the word *being*: the word which language shelters by hiding it, or causes to appear when language itself disappears into the silent void of the work" (22). The writer's relation to the work arises out of his or her inability to bring it to expression, which becomes an affirmation of the work's solitude and disappearance.

Blanchot explains that the writer grapples with certain illusions about the ability to write, or to produce work. With words at his or her disposal, the writer sometimes feels mastery over language, manipulating it as a tool of expression. "But his mastery only succeeds in putting him, keeping him in contact with the fundamental passivity where the word, no longer anything but its appearance—the shadow of a word—never can be mastered or even grasped" (25). Blanchot uses the example of a writer who clings to a pencil, not able to let it go, but also not able to grasp it. The hand that writes cannot stop writing because it engages in an incessant movement where it does not have the power to stop. The writing hand (Blanchot calls it the "sick hand") depends upon the other, masterful, hand to interrupt the writing—to seize the pencil in its empowered grasp and to put an end to that which has no beginning or end. In this way, the mastery of the writer does not consist of writing, but of the power to stop writing. This mastery betrays the infinite movement of the work, bringing it out of the realm of shadows, but also, in doing so, marking the moment of its essential disappearance. Turning away from the approach to the work, in an act of betrayal (Blanchot will later call it impatience), the writer reveals the impossibility of the work, its refusal and exclusion of both writer and reader. And so the writer returns to work:

> The obsession which ties him to a privileged theme which obliges him to say over again what he has already said [. . .] illustrates the necessity, which apparently determines his efforts, that he always come back to the same point, pass again over the same paths, persevere in starting over what for him never starts, and that he belong to the shadow of events, not their reality, to their image, not the object, to what allows words themselves to become images, appearances—not signs, values, the power of truth. (24)

The interruption of the writing does not cure the sickness, but suspends it, affirming the impossibility of the task and the interminability of the process.

One way in which Blanchot considers the decisive moment when writing stops, if only to start again, concerns the distinction of the book and the work. The writer opens himself or herself to the approach of the work, relinquishing power and activity, risking solitude and disappearance—but this movement is ultimately substituted by the book. "The writer belongs to the work, but what belongs to him is only a book, a mute collection of sterile words, the most insignificant thing in the world" (23). The writer produces the book, and, faced with the inadequacy of the book, he or she returns to writing, hoping that a little more time and effort will complete the task. For Blanchot, the writer's illusion, or powerlessness to stop trying, remains important because it sends him or her back to work, even if "what he wants to finish by himself remains interminable" (23). While the book can have significance in the world, as the material or worldly aspect of the work, it has nothing to do with the writer's approach to the work, which eludes signification; yet the book remains, paradoxically, as the only evidence of the writer's task. John Gregg provides insight into the relationship of the book and the work in *The Literature of Transgression*:

> The work, on the other hand, escapes comprehension. It contains an inexhaustible reserve that can never be completely explained away, accounted for, or summed up by interpretation. The "evidence of the book" seems to be a solid structure, but it is an edifice built on the ever-shifting sands of the work. The lack of solid foundation accounts for the inadequation of the work with itself, which Blanchot calls "the absence of the book." [. . .] The work is and is not there. Its constant movement is an oscillation between apparition and disappearance [. . .].[11]

The work exceeds the limits of the book; it does not appear anywhere in the book. But this excessiveness remains at the heart of the book, as the book's inability to contain it or to do away with it—to make it appear or disappear. The book remains as that which is available to comprehension, and, for this reason, refuses the reading of the work. Blanchot suggests, though, that this refusal and the non-coincidence of book and work provide a space of rupture where the disappearance or concealment of the work might paradoxically come forward, as that which must remain hidden. He approaches this subject first by considering the writer's attempt to read his or her work.

In the face of the inability to finish the task of writing, or to bring forth the work in anything other than a book, the writer might decide to approach the book as a reader. In doing so, the writer confronts "the abrupt *Noli me legere*," experiencing inability for a second time. Blanchot tells us that "the writer never reads his work. It is for him illegible, a secret" (24).[12] But he also clarifies that the refusal, the *Noli me legere*, establishes the writer's relation with the work.

> It is not the force of an interdict, but, through the play and sense of words, the insistent, the rude and poignant affirmation that what is there, in the global presence of a definitive text, still withholds itself—the rude and biting void of refusal—or excludes, with the authority of indifference, him who, having written it, yet wants to grasp it afresh by reading it. (25)

The moment when the writer faces that which turns him or her away, that which affirms concealment, recalls the characterization of the work as the appearance of "everything has disappeared." The writer, in his or her attempted approach as reader, experiences the depth of this concealment—a depth that otherwise remains unapproachable to the writer during the patient efforts to continue working. The *Noli me legere* affirms the disappearance of the work, if only for a moment, since the writer ultimately returns to work with no choice but to do so. We might imagine the sick hand again, especially since Blanchot describes the writer's approach to the text as reader in terms of the desire to "grasp it afresh by reading it." The sick hand grasps the pencil, unable to let it go, but in doing so, as we saw earlier, exposes the writer to "the fundamental passivity where the word, no longer anything but its appearance—the shadow of a word—never can be mastered or even grasped" (25). While grasping first suggests power and understanding, it reveals itself as a sort of passive movement that stems from inability. The desire to read, for the writer, reflects the loss or absence involved in his or her task, since it would ideally serve to recover what has disappeared, or has receded beyond the grasp of the writer in his or her approach to the work. The writer attempts to read with mastery, and in doing so encounters a refusal that constitutes his or her only relation to the work.

In Blanchot's thought, the writer clearly does not operate from a position of ability or mastery, but rather slips into a movement where the power to speak, to say "I," disappears. "To write, moreover, is to withdraw language from the world, to detach it from what makes it a power according to which, when I speak, it is the world that declares itself, the clear light of day that develops through tasks undertaken, through action and time" (26). Writing turns language over to the movement of the work, which lacks time and exceeds the activity and comprehension of the world. And the turning over, or withdrawing of language, which is writing, also opens a space for writing. This space becomes a risk to the writer, who no longer inhabits the realm illuminated by the light of day, where language signifies the power to express oneself and the truth of the world. Not only does writing withdraw language from the world, but it also withdraws the writer from the world—again, not in the sense that the task of writing requires that the writer seclude himself or herself from the daily activity of the world. Rather, the writer is pulled into the dark of withdrawn language, where he or she can make nothing appear or disappear through language, including the "I."

> The writer belongs to a language which no one speaks, which is addressed to no one, which has no center, and which reveals nothing. He may believe that he affirms himself in this language, but what he affirms is altogether deprived of self. To the extent that, being a writer, he does justice to what requires writing, he can never again express himself, or even introduce another's speech. Where he is, only being speaks—which means that language doesn't speak anymore, but is. It devotes itself to the pure passivity of being. (26-27)

Blanchot clarifies that the language of writing has nothing to do with claims of universality or objectivity; it does not signify the writer's sacrifice of a subjective, personal voice in favor of one that attempts to speak a more general truth. Writing withdraws language away from a relation with truth, light, or understanding, and the writer's sacrifice takes on a much different character—a sacrifice of the ability to speak, and thus to say "I." Blanchot writes, "The third person substituting for the 'I': such is the solitude that comes to the writer on account of the work. [. . .] The third person is myself become no one, my interlocutor turned alien [. . .]" (28). In this case, the "third person" does not suggest a character, a carefully developed "he" who one might imagine finding in the world; the third person indicates no one, a voice that rises out of the inability to speak.[13]

When considering that the writer belongs to a language where he or she doesn't have the power to speak, we can begin to sense the risk of disappearance that the writer confronts in the process of writing. Blanchot briefly touches upon the tendency of writers to keep a journal because he believes it reveals the writer's suspicion of his or her disappearance in the impersonality of the work.[14] When faced with anonymity, the writer often takes up writing of a different sort—one which might re-establish the writer's place in the world, as an "I." Blanchot calls the journal a "memorial," suggesting that the writer seeks to remember what has been lost, perhaps in an effort to salvage something of this "I." Of course, the writer problematically turns to language in order to overcome the withdrawal of language, and the exposure of the "I" to this withdrawal, which would seem to reveal the futility of the effort. But Blanchot proposes that the interest of the journal lies in its deliberate references to the mundane events of everyday life and the writer's participation in this life. The writer is grasping:

> Here, true things are still spoken of. Here, whoever speaks retains his name and speaks in this name, and the dates he notes down belong in a shared time when what happens really happens. The journal—this book which is apparently altogether solitary—is often written out of fear and anguish at the solitude which comes to the writer on account of the work. (29)

In his or her disappearance, the writer turns to the journal almost in an act of denial. In the journal, the writer believes him or herself to be able to speak, to say "I," to belong to the present—that which the experience of the work refuses.

We might ask what it is about language that exposes the writer to the disappearance of himself or herself and the work. In *The Space of Literature*, Blanchot turns to Mallarmé as a means of exploring this question. I would first like briefly to turn to an earlier essay, "Literature and the Right to Death," in order to consider the way that Blanchot characterizes the role of disappearance, or negativity, in language and literature. He writes:

> Hölderlin, Mallarmé, and all poets whose theme is the essence of poetry have felt that the act of naming is disquieting and marvelous. A word may give me its meaning, but first it suppresses it. For me to be able to say, "This woman" I must somehow take her flesh and blood reality away from her, cause her to be absent, annihilate her. The word gives me the being, but it gives it to me deprived of being. The word is the absence of that being, its nothingness, what is left of it when it has lost being—the very fact that it does not exist.[15]

Blanchot is referring to Hegel's discussion of language in *The Phenomenology of the Spirit*, which is a continual point of reference throughout the essay.[16] A word must make what it names disappear, precisely in order to name it; this act of negation gives rise to the appearance of an idea, or a concept, which replaces that which has disappeared. Common language assumes that the woman (in this case) whom language negates can re-appear in the idea, which is given by the word "woman." The word thus expresses the idea, fulfilling, and disappearing in, its communicative function. In this way, not only does everyday language involve the disappearance of that which it names, but also of language itself; its efficiency as a communicative tool would seem to depend upon a certain assumption of, and interest in, transparency. But in the passage above, Blanchot emphasizes the lingering absence, the loss of being, that necessarily arises in this process. The word points to the absence or disappearance of what it designates, what has been sacrificed for the appearance of the idea. Blanchot focuses upon the woman's death, rather than her recovery—a death at the heart of that which remains, because it (death) has paradoxically become the condition for the woman's existence, despite her absence.

In the previous passage, Blanchot notes the poet's interest in the "disquieting and marvelous" power of naming—its ability to put to death in order to create the world. Instead of looking past death, the poet makes it the concern of the work; rather than accepting the act of naming as a constructive activity that provides meaning, the language of literature brings attention to what has disappeared, precisely by demonstrating its disappearance. Blanchot writes:

> When literature refuses to name anything, when it turns a name into something obscure and meaningless, witness to the primordial obscurity, what has disappeared in this case—the meaning of the name—is really destroyed, but signification in general has appeared in its place, the meaning of the meaninglessness embedded in the word as expression of the obscurity of existence, so that although the precise meaning of the terms has faded, what asserts itself now is the very possibility of signifying, the empty power of bestowing meaning—a strange impersonal light. (385)

Literature's refusal to name thus involves the obfuscation of the name, which negates the ability of the name to make something appear. Now, nothing appears—both in the sense that literature's negation is not constructive, and also, in the sense that nothingness, the "empty power of bestowing meaning," appears as the movement of disappearance, which is unable to make itself disappear. After the negation of the world and the name, negation confronts its own excessive persistence. In his essay "Crossing the Threshold: Literature and the Right to Death," Christopher Fynsk discusses this moment: "The inability to avoid signifying, become the 'empty power [of bestowing meaning],' is the expression of the 'powerlessness to disappear' of the being of what is before the day, the existence from which one must turn away to speak and to understand."[17] In this way, the power of signification, negation, or disappearance (which work as synonyms here), reaches the point of its powerlessness to deal with itself, and thus expresses that which precedes and exceeds its power—the "primordial obscurity" from which it is always and necessarily turned away.

Returning to *The Space of Literature*, Blanchot's discussion of Mallarmé engages many of the reflections developed in "Literature and the Right to Death." The earlier essay can help elucidate Blanchot's approach to Mallarmé's exploration of language and poetry. Blanchot traces the "experience" of Mallarmé, as he does with a number of writers who continually emerge throughout his work. His discussion of these writers emerges as something closer to a conversation than a definitive critique where he takes a stand for or against what seems to be proposed by the writer. It is sometimes even hard to tell who is speaking—Blanchot, or the writer with whom he is conversing, or neither—as the voice of the text often seems to float between vague citations, developments, commentary, and questioning. This mode of writing becomes especially apparent in Blanchot's later works, like *The Infinite Conversation*, but I would argue that his conversations with Mallarmé, Kafka, Rilke, and Hölderlin in *The Space of Literature* already demonstrate the deliberate un-grounding of the voice of the text. In these conversations, Blanchot explores the various contradictions and difficulties that arise with attempts to respond to the demand and to the question of literature, emphasizing the persistence and the inexhaustibility of both the demand and the question.

Blanchot begins by considering some of Mallarmé's early attempts to define "essential," or literary, language, and to distinguish it from "crude" language. He explains that Mallarmé understands both crude and essential language in terms of their respective relations to silence. The crude word is "silent [. . .] because meaningless"; it designates the language of everyday exchange and functions within the "reality" of the world (*SL* 39). It seeks to make things appear, and to make them present to us—without mediation, or, in other words, as if language transparently expressed the idea or concept. Like Blanchot, Mallarmé is interested in the way that negativity functions in language, and he brings attention to what necessarily disappears in the act of naming. But Mallarmé's characterization of crude language focuses on the assumption of what it can make appear; the role of silence, in the case of everyday language, refers to the way that language itself disappears into its function—"language as language is silent" (40). On the other hand, the essential word indicates a language "whose whole force lies in its not being, whose very glory is to evoke, in its own absence, the absence of everything" (39). Rather than relying on the power of language to make things appear, essential language exposes their disappearance—the silence of the world. "It is always allusive. It suggests, it evokes" (39). Unlike the crude word, the essential word does not function as a tool in the world, relying on generalizations in order to name and identify things, in the interest of communication and understanding.[18] "Poetry expresses the fact that beings are silent" (41). But, here, we encounter a problem: if silence is the essence of essential language, then it would seem that everyday language touches upon this essence, in the sense that it must, like essential language, silence the world in order to name and designate things, even if it pretends otherwise. In other words, the crude word might at first seem only to silence language (because it encourages us to look through or past it), but it relies upon the essential silence *of* language in order to function, despite its efforts to hide it. The distinction of the crude word and the essential word by their relation to silence thus becomes problematic. Blanchot writes of the crude word: "A word which does not name anything, which does not represent anything, which does not outlast itself in any way, a word which is not even a word and which disappears marvelously altogether and at once in its usage: what could be more worthy of the essential and closer to silence?" (39-40). Since, as Blanchot demonstrates in "Literature and the Right to Death," everyday language presents the absence of what it has made disappear, it does "[express] the fact that beings are silent," just like essential language—perhaps even more essentially, precisely because it pretends otherwise, because it attempts to hide this absence. It seems that the distinction of crude and essential language relies on the ability of the crude word to make the concept appear, to make it immediate to us; this veils the more "essential" silence at work. Blanchot continues, "[. . .] it is nothingness in action: that which acts, labors, constructs. It is the pure silence of the negative which culminates in the noisy feverishness of tasks" (40). This usefulness, the activity of crude language in the world, does seem to distinguish it from essential language, in the sense that the latter separates itself from the labor of the world; but Blanchot draws attention to the way that everyday language merely presents the illusion of immediacy and actually hides within it the silence that characterizes Mallarmé's notion of essential language.

After exploring the questions that arise with the definition of crude language, Blanchot turns to the way that essential language figures into Mallarmé's thought. It would seem that the uselessness of essential language, its separation from the labor of the world, would take it out of the realm of constructive negativity; essential language makes no claim to signify and to make appear things in the world. In crude language, language is silent and beings speak. In essential language, "beings fall silent" (41). Blanchot then takes us to the next step in Mallarmé's thought:

> The poetic word is no longer someone's word. In it no one speaks, and what speaks is not anyone. It seems rather that the word alone declares itself. Then language takes on all of its importance. It becomes essential. Language speaks as the essential, and that is why the word entrusted to the poet can be called the essential word. [. . .] From this perspective, we rediscover poetry as a powerful universe of words where relations, configurations, forces are affirmed through sound, figure, rhythmic mobility, in a unified and sovereignly autonomous space. (41-42)

While the first part of this passage might recall Blanchot's discussion of the neutral voice, the "third person substituting for the 'I,'" it soon takes a decisive turn. In a sense, the power of the poet is exchanged for the power of language; in this formulation, the poet does not use language as a means of expressing himself or herself, or the world, but relies upon the language of the poem, as a self-contained totality, to bring itself to light. We already know that, for Blanchot, writing has nothing to do with power, but begins at the point of power's exhaustion. For Mallarmé, it seems that the poem is able to make itself appear, to exist, through essential language. The poet *constructs* something out of absence and silence, even if it has no voice, and if no one speaks it; therefore, from this perspective, writing does not differ from the activity—the constructive negativity—of the world. The lack of voice seems to reflect the poem's autonomy and separation from the world (including the poet perhaps), rather than a more radical turning toward silence and disappearance, in which it would lose itself. For Blanchot, at this point in Mallarmé's thought, the poem remains "a particular being [. . .] and for this reason is by no means close to being, to that which escapes all determination and every form of existence" (42). The poem, as a thing or a being, still misses a more essential movement towards its own disappearance.[19]

Blanchot proposes that the "experience proper" of Mallarmé begins at the point when "he moves from the consideration of a finished work which is always one particular poem or another, or a certain picture, to the concern through which the work becomes the search for its origin and wants to identify itself with this origin" (42). Writing becomes a question for Mallarmé—the question of whether or not it exists, and the implications of such a question. The poem, as a linguistically manifest "thing," would seem to affirm the existence of poetry, and, furthermore, the poet's work would presumably require the writing of poetry. Even if essential language silences the world and the poet, even if it says nothing, the poem, as a thing, appears. But what, exactly, appears? And does that which appears have anything to do with the work? After all, Blanchot has already told us that Mallarmé falters when he thinks of a poem as a being, which would suggest that poems do not exist—at least not in the sense that we commonly understand things in the world to exist. It's as if once the poem exists, poetry ceases to exist; once the poem arrives at the appearance of itself, as the work of poetry, it is lost. Blanchot insists on maintaining the openness and the endlessness of the question of literature, which is assured by the infinite self-referentiality of language and by the impossibility of arriving at the origin that would assure its existence. Blanchot explains, "[language] is wholly realized in literature, which is to say that it has only the reality of the whole; it is all—and nothing else, always on the verge of passing from all to nothing" (43). Literature takes us to the point of language's accomplishment—a point that it realizes through a movement of negation, or disappearance. But this point of accomplishment, of wholeness, becomes a point of passage; as language achieves its own end, through the power to the make the world and itself disappear, it reaches its limit, where it passes from all to nothing. And, paradoxically, it is at this "end point" that literature begins, or starts over, in a time without time, where nothing appears, and where we can no longer measure the accomplishment of anything. Blanchot describes this as the "central point" of the literary experience: "This point is the one at which complete realization of language coincides with its disappearance" (44). Once completely realized, yet still lacking, language disappears into the superfluous movement of disappearance itself.

Blanchot considers the ambiguous "central point" of the work more closely once he has posed the question of literature as an endless search for its origin. He cites Mallarmé, writing that "the work must 'allow no luminous evidence except of existing'" (44). The darkness allows nothing to appear, maintaining only the movement of negation and absence. Blanchot continues:

It is very true that only the work—if we come toward this point through the movement and strength of the work—only the accomplishment of the work makes it possible. Let us look again at the poem: what could be more real, more evident? And language itself is "luminous evidence" within it. This evidence, however, shows nothing, rests upon nothing; it is the ungraspable in action. There are neither terms nor moments. Where we think we have words, "a virtual trail of fires" shoots through us—a swiftness, a scintillating exaltation. A reciprocity: for what is not is revealed in this flight; what there isn't is reflected in the pure grace of reflections that do not reflect anything. (44-45)

The work takes us to the point of its accomplishment, and therefore to the central point of the work. We arrive at the moment where the word, after turning itself over completely to darkness, seems to emerge as "luminous evidence." But Blanchot explains that this evidence makes nothing evident; the words only reflect each other in an endless chain of signifiers that grounds itself in nothing. The moment of accomplishment therefore reveals the inability to grasp or take hold of anything that would assure it. Language opens onto that which cannot be negated, accomplished, or made to appear, precisely at the moment of its completion. "What is left? 'Those very words, *it is*'" (45, emphasis in original).

Mallarmé describes that residual pronouncement—*it is*—as a "'lightning moment,' 'dazzling burst of light'" (45, cited by Blanchot). The work reaches the central point of the work, where, after the negation of everything, nothing exists; but at this moment of brilliant achievement, the work simultaneously experiences its undoing. Blanchot writes, "This moment is the one at which the work, in order to give being to the 'feint'—that 'literature exists'—declares the exclusion of everything, but in this way, excludes itself, so that the moment at which 'every reality dissolves' by the force of the poem is also the moment the poem dissolves and, instantly done, is instantly undone" (45). And yet still for Blanchot this formulation does not quite reach the moment of radical reversal that makes the work impossible. Here, in Mallarmé's words, the undoing of the work also constitutes the ultimate achievement of the work—the point at which it disappears in the movement of disappearance it has accomplished. "Those very words *it is*" appear as the extreme possibility of the work, even if only for a brilliant moment.[20] This point marks the work as "pure beginning," since the accomplishment of the work gives rise to the *it is*—the light of being that disappears at the moment it begins. But, Blanchot explains, "we must also comprehend and feel that this point renders the work impossible, because it never permits arrival at the work. It is a region anterior to the beginning where nothing is made of being, and in which nothing is ever accomplished" (46). The work exceeds the ability of the work to begin, which prevents its accomplishment and its initiation. Writing takes us toward the central point, toward the origin of the work—from which it issues, but also from which it is infinitely excluded. For this reason, the task of the work remains endless and impossible, but this condition sustains the work in the movement that characterizes it—a search for a beginning that cannot possibly begin. Disappearance, then, does not refer to an ideal moment where being momentarily pronounces itself in the absence of everything; rather, disappearance becomes the stubborn refusal of anything to appear, to begin, to be—even itself.

At the central point of his own work, Blanchot reflects upon the myth of Orpheus and Eurydice and the way that this myth recounts the infinite search for the work's origin. Orpheus's journey toward Eurydice demonstrates the power of art to open the nothingness of the underworld at the same time that it confronts the moment of the work's impossibility and undoing. From the perspective of the world, Orpheus, in his impatience, fails to bring Eurydice to the light of day, but Blanchot suggests that Orpheus *must* fail in order not to fail the work. Orpheus's betrayal and loss of Eurydice becomes a sort of faithfulness to the work, even if this faithfulness can only be achieved through a turning away. Blanchot explains that Eurydice "is the profoundly obscure point toward which art and desire, death and night, seem to tend. She is the instant when the essence of night approaches as the *other* night" (171). And, here, we can imagine that the obscurity of this point only becomes more obscure in the approach to it. If the first night—the space of the empowered descent toward Eurydice—maintains a certain clarity in its darkness, and promises the possibility of Eurydice's retrieval, the *other* night looms in the distance, at the point where the power and possibility of art to make anything appear are exhausted.

Orpheus is capable of everything, except of looking this point in the face, except of looking at the center of night in the night. He can descend toward it; he can—and this is still stronger an ability—draw it to him and lead it with him upward, but only by turning away from it. This turning away is the only way it can be approached. This is what concealment means when it reveals itself in the night. But Orpheus, in the movement of his migration, forgets the work he is to achieve, and he forgets it necessarily, for the ultimate demand which his movement makes is not that there be a work, but that someone face this point, grasp its essence, grasp it where it appears, where it is essential and essentially appearance: at the heart of night. (171)

From this perspective, it seems that the ability to see poses the greatest threat to the work, and the turning away of one's vision, in a sort of blind and backwards approach to the work, becomes the extreme expression of the artist's ability. Concealment, here, rests upon the artist's power to resist looking, and therefore arises out of the masterful patience of the artist. But, in order for there to be a work, one must eventually look, in an effort to see and to grasp the essence of the night. This moment marks the disappearance of the work, in the most profound concealment, which, paradoxically, responds to the ultimate demand of the work.

At the point when Orpheus looks back, Eurydice recedes beyond his grasp, and he loses her forever. He fails to bring her back up to the light and the world, despite his power to transgress the normal limits of human endeavor by opening the depths of Hades with his song. Orpheus achieves miraculous feats, accomplishes all that can be accomplished, but the myth tells us of his ultimate failure. His look back to Eurydice not only marks the moment of Orpheus's failure to retrieve her, but also disposes of the value of the journey he makes to get to that point; in losing Eurydice, the journey is ruined. Blanchot writes:

> When he looks back, the essence of the night is revealed as the inessential. Thus he betrays the work, and Eurydice, and the night. But not to turn toward Eurydice would be no less untrue. Not to look would be infidelity to the measureless, imprudent force of his movement, which does not want Eurydice in her daytime truth and everyday appeal, but wants her in her

nocturnal obscurity, in her distance, with her closed body and sealed face—wants to see her not when she is visible, but when she is invisible, and not as the intimacy of a familiar life, but as the foreignness of what excludes all intimacy, and wants, not to make her live, but to have living in her the plenitude of death. (172)

The work requires that Orpheus not look if he wants to bring it to a successful conclusion. But the work also requires Orpheus to look, in the sense that his loss of Eurydice, his experience of her disappearance, affirms her obscurity, concealment, and infinite recession beyond his grasp. If Orpheus seems to have the power to retrieve Eurydice, to make her appear again in the world, it would rest upon his ability to transform her into something he does not seek and that has little to do with his work. Orpheus cannot capture the nocturnal Eurydice by making her visible, so he must look, in order to experience the only relation he can have with her—one based on her invisibility and her disappearance. Orpheus seeks Eurydice in her profound absence; when he looks, he does not experience her absence in a "lightning moment" that marks the accomplishment of the work, but, rather, confronts the depth of her concealment and refusal to appear.

Blanchot's discussion of patience and impatience as it relates to Orpheus's descent and ultimate look back at Eurydice demonstrates the resistance of his reading of the myth to dialectical understanding. Blanchot often describes the writer as a sort of wanderer whose work consists of an interminable, undirected movement, rather than an arrival at a final destination. This fits with the notion that the writer disappears into an anonymous, neutral space where he or she no longer operates from a place of power, individuality, or decisiveness. As we saw earlier, the writer's mastery has nothing to do with an ability to write, but, rather, refers to the capacity to interrupt the errant and unending process of writing—to the moment when he or she decides to stop writing. The work would seem to require infinite patience from the writer, since it pulls him or her into a space and a process without a horizon and demands that he or she sustain an endless movement. But in order to have *a* work, and in order to confront the ultimate refusal of the work, the writer commits an act of impatience, an interruption, a look back. As Orpheus descends into the Underworld, he must exhibit patience, submitting to the law that forbids him to look back at Eurydice until she returns to the light of day. And the myth encourages us to imagine that if he sustained this patient movement while drawing Eurydice upwards, he would succeed in having her again, with him, in the world. But he can't keep himself from looking:

> Orpheus is guilty of impatience. His error is to want to exhaust the infinite, to put a term to the interminable, not endlessly to sustain the very movement of his error. Impatience is the failing of one who wants to withdraw from the absence of time; patience is the ruse which seeks to master this absence by making of it another time, measured otherwise. But true patience does not exclude impatience. It is intimacy with impatience—impatience suffered and endured endlessly. (173)

Blanchot shifts our attention from what the myth seems to present as a possibility—resurrecting Eurydice—to the impossibility of Orpheus's essential work. The myth suggests that Orpheus's task has a goal and an end point; there is presumably nothing infinite about it. But, again, this goal does not inspire Orpheus; that which inspires Orpheus requires an endlessly sustained movement—one where nothing can be accomplished or achieved. Therefore, his act of impatience responds to his desire to see Eurydice in her nocturnal state, rather than maintaining the interval and the infinite movement by keeping himself turned away.

While we might be tempted to conclude that Orpheus's impatience results in his failure, and that patience would have guaranteed his success, we have already seen that success, from the perspective of the world, would not satisfy Orpheus's work. In addition, in the passage above, Blanchot refers to patience as a "ruse" which is no more faithful to the absence of time than impatience. Infinite patience would fail to take Orpheus to the point where the work experiences its undoing—a point where it is exposed to the absence of time and to the excess of disappearance when everything has disappeared. Orpheus's patient descent still requires a certain degree of mastery, and his look back marks the limit of his power; at this limit, he confronts a refusal that constitutes his relation with the work. His look back announces an end, and it also announces a beginning that cannot possibly begin. In this look, Orpheus experiences his own disappearance, along with the disappearance of Eurydice. He no longer has the power to speak, to sing, to say "I," or to make anything appear in the light of day. Therefore, while we might at first see the moment of impatience as an empowered interruption of the interminable process of the work, it also marks the release of the work beyond its relation with Orpheus and his song. And, for Blanchot, this represents a moment of inspiration: "To look at Eurydice, without regard for the song, in the impatience and imprudence of desire which forgets the law: *that is inspiration*" (173, emphasis in original). Orpheus sacrifices everything in a reckless moment where his power to master the night disintegrates, and he experiences the profound disappearance of what his song seemed to have within its grasp. "But that forbidden movement is precisely what Orpheus must accomplish in order to carry the work beyond what assures it" (174). Orpheus's look sends the work infinitely away, to disappear beyond a space where things can be made to disappear. Paradoxically, Blanchot explains that Orpheus must have already looked back in order to initiate his descent toward Eurydice. Orpheus enters the night through the seductive power of his song—a song that begins at the moment he turns back toward Eurydice to bring her in her absence to the light of day. His loss of Eurydice becomes the song, which always refers back to the loss of what inspires it. Orpheus's work is the means by which he initiates his work, and this circularity reflects the absence of time of the work. The interminable error of the writer's process, even if interrupted by an impatient look back, is maintained precisely in the impossibility encountered by the look back—the impossibility of beginning or ending. Blanchot explains, "One writes only if one reaches that instant which nevertheless one can only approach in the space opened by the movement of writing. To write, one has to write already" (176).

In one of the last sections of *The Space of Literature*, Blanchot turns his attention to the act of reading and its relation to writing. If writing depends upon a movement toward disappearance, loss, and impossibility, reading would seem to counter this movement in some sense. Blanchot often describes reading as a light and careless process, which strongly contrasts the serious risk involved in the task of writing. And, yet, reading plays a crucial role in the "life" of the book. "What is a book no one reads? Something that is not yet written. It would seem, then, that to read is not to write the book again, but to allow the book to *be*: written—this time all by itself, without the intermediary of the writer, without anyone's writing it. The reader does not add himself to the book, but tends primarily to relieve it of its author" (193). Here, it is important to note that Blanchot is discussing the book, not the work—one that a reader might or might not open, depending on his or her mood or some other extraneous factor. But this lack of care or investment brings a sort of freedom to the book, which, without the reader, remains weighted down in its relation to the writer. Even if the work pulls the writer into a space of powerlessness and takes him or her toward disappearance, the book bears the traces of this grave struggle until the reader calls it forward and relieves it of its author. And if the work demands that the writer disappear into anonymity, the reader responds to this demand by picking up the book, without regard for the writer, as if this writer had no relation to what is written. Blanchot explains that this reader could be any reader:

> The reader is himself always fundamentally anonymous. He is any reader, none in particular, unique but transparent. He does not add his name to the book (as our fathers did long ago); rather, he erases every name from it by his nameless presence, his modest, passive gaze, interchangeable and insignificant, under whose light pressure the book appears written, separate from everything and everyone. (193)

In this passage, we see that the reader's anonymity parallels the writer's, and the use of the word "gaze" perhaps suggests the myth of Orpheus. While writer and reader have distinct relations to the book (and to the work), Blanchot deliberately blurs the distinction at points in order to emphasize the way that the two processes mirror one another, never really sustaining a stable identity or role of their own. The reader's anonymity suggests that the act of relieving the book from its author does not constitute a moment of power or mastery, where the reader makes the book his or her own. At this point, reading is simply a matter of carelessly gazing at the book; and though this gaze casually seeks to make something appear, it certainly does not experience the profound loss associated with the writer's gaze. The writer's anonymity, on the other hand, refers to a sort of sacrifice demanded by the work. And when the writer "gazes" in a moment of impatience, he or she loses everything and affirms the disappearance and concealment of the work. But even when recounting the myth of Orpheus, Blanchot continually comes back to the notion of the carelessness and lightness of impatience—the way that the sacrifice of the work and the look back to Eurydice require a moment where the writer forgets all the work, effort and patience that led him or her to that point. In the look back, the writer seems to act more like a reader, or even to respond to reading's demand.

While the reader first approaches the book in a state of disappearance where he or she has no particular identity, reading soon seems to have a mission. In reading's approach to the book, something becomes apparent: "The book is there, then, but the work is still hidden. It is absent, perhaps radically so; in any case, it is concealed, obfuscated by the evident presence of the book, behind which it awaits the liberating decision, the 'Lazare, veni foras'" (195). This reference to Jesus's resurrecting call to Lazarus evokes Blanchot's earlier use of the command *Noli me legere*, which plays off of Jesus's warning to Mary that she not touch him. Whereas *Noli me legere* represents a refusal—particularly the denial of the writer when he or she tries to read the work—*Lazare veni foras* would seem to suggest the reader's power to make something appear in his or her approach to the book. The reader, who first opens the book in anonymity and lightness, soon experiences the book as the concealment of the absent work. Blanchot continues: "To make this stone fall seems to be reading's mission: to render it transparent, to dissolve it with the penetrating force of the gaze which unimpeded moves beyond" (195). And reading thus calls forth the work, seeking to make it appear from behind the stone, through the power of its gaze. If the reader's gaze was light and casual at first, it now takes on the seriousness of a task. And where Orpheus fails (in the sense that his gaze and attempt to resurrect Eurydice send her infinitely away), Jesus succeeds in bringing the dead Lazarus back to life. It would seem that reading has become the power to make absence appear.

Blanchot further explores the resurrecting power of reading by examining the significance of the speaking, breathing Lazarus:

> To roll back the stone, to obliterate it, is certainly something marvelous, but it is something we achieve at every moment in everyday language. [. . .] In his well-woven winding sheet, sustained by the most elegant conventions, [Lazarus] answers us and speaks to us within ourselves. But what answers the call of literary reading is not a door falling open or becoming transparent or even getting a bit thinner. It is, rather, a ruder stone, better sealed, a crushing weight, an immense avalanche that causes earth and sky to shudder. (195)

Picking up the book, the reader becomes aware of the presence of the massive stone that hides the work and seeks to get beyond this stone by beckoning the work to appear. And in the Biblical story, Lazarus indeed emerges from behind the stone once again to take part in the world of the living. Blanchot, though, compares the resurrection of Lazarus to everyday language, which causes us to reconsider the significance of what is made to appear. Everyday language negates what it names in order to give rise to the concept, but what appears bears the absence of what has disappeared in the act of naming. Lazarus, then, appears—but as a sort of replacement or stand-in for what has been called forth from behind the stone; moreover, this resurrected Lazarus appears as the profound concealment of the dead Lazarus. One has to kill the already dead Lazarus in order to bring him into the light of day, and the resurrected Lazarus paradoxically bears the death of the dead Lazarus at the same time that he hides it by appearing alive, cleanly clothed, and full of life. In *The Infinite Conversation*, Blanchot continues his reflections on the resurrection of Lazarus:

> But what does this Lazarus saved and raised from the dead that you hold out to me have to do with what is lying there and makes you draw back, the anonymous corruption of the tomb, the lost Lazarus who already smells bad and not the one restored to life by a force that is no doubt admirable, but that is precisely a force and that comes in this decision from death itself? (36)

Although the story of Lazarus's resurrection at first seems to contrast the myth of Orpheus, Blanchot encourages us to see the calling forth of Lazarus in terms of constructive negativity. While Lazarus appears, through the force of a marvelous power, he announces the absence of what remains concealed.

Returning specifically to the relation of the Lazarus story to reading, we can see that reading's mission to "roll back the stone" might indeed result in the successful appearance of Lazarus in the world, but that this appearance points to a profound disappearance. Blanchot tells us that "what answers the call of literary reading is not a door falling open or becoming transparent or even getting a bit thinner. It is, rather, a ruder stone, better sealed, a crushing weight, an immense avalanche that causes earth and sky to shudder" (195). Even though the reader calls forth the work, Blanchot shifts our attention from what seems to be resurrected to the "ruder stone" that refuses the reader's call and power to make appear. The apocalyptic language of Blanchot's description suggests that the stone marks an extreme limit—the end of everything—and that the dead Lazarus lies beyond, and in excess of, this end. In this way, the reader's relation to the work does not differ from that of the writer; both confront the refusal of the work, even if the reader's interpretive efforts might give the appearance of bringing the mysteries of the book to life. John Gregg explains, "Thus the *noli me legere* which Blanchot consistently invokes to describe writers' incapability of authoritatively reading their own works, actually applies to all readers. No one can read the work. It is the book that lends itself to understanding, and it can be read by both author and reader."[21] Like the writer, the reader does not have the power to make the work appear; both can approach the book, but the work always escapes the grasp of this approach. For this reason, the lightness, carelessness, and anonymity of the reader's process become the essential aspect of his or her relation to the work, in the sense that these characteristics contrast a sort of reading that would seek to impose an authoritative interpretation. It must be added, though, that the interpretive efforts of a reader confront the refusal of the work, and therefore affirm the disappearance of the work and constitute the reader's only relation to the work. Again, Blanchot keeps us from being able absolutely to distinguish "good" reading from "bad" reading, ability from inability, calling forth from letting be. In this particular case, the calling forth of the book into the light of day, although it makes of reading an act of power, also affirms the disappearance of the work. Blanchot writes, "Disappearance, even when it is disguised as useful presence, belongs to the work's essence" (206). Reading thus parallels the gaze of Orpheus, which paradoxically remains faithful to the work by betraying it.

Toward the end of *The Space of Literature*, Blanchot returns to a reflection on ends, on the final moment where the world's truth appears through the labor of man and the process of history:

> When all has been said, when the world comes into its own as the truth of the whole, when history wants to culminate in the conclusion of discourse—when the work has nothing more to say and disappears—it is then that it tends to become the language of the work. In the work that has disappeared the work wants to speak, and the experience of the work becomes the search for its essence, the affirmation of art, concern for the origin. (232)

In the chapters that follow, I will explore the way that several short fictions reflect the language of the disappeared work—a language that doesn't have the ability to begin, or appear, or speak. Writer and reader communicate with this unspeakable language and face the threat of their own disappearance at the point that they turn over the power to bring their work forward into the light of day. All of the fictions address a space where, in one way or another, nothing can be done and nothing can be made to appear. In this way, they explore the dynamics of disappearance and the way that this movement of infinite recession characterizes the literary work.

Chapter 2: Franz Kafka and the Disappearance of the Writer

One of the tricky questions that confronts us when reading the narratives of Franz Kafka concerns the difficulty of making any sort of assertion about meanings, allegorical implications, or the act of interpretation in general. It seems too easy to find oneself in the trap of suggesting an underlying truth or transcendent principle to guide our reading; critics such as Walter Benjamin and Gilles Deleuze have famously and correctly exposed the limitations of such readings. And yet a limited approach feels difficult to escape. Perhaps the temptation to "read for meaning"—insofar as that act threatens to be dangerously reductive, if unavoidable—begins with the sense that Kafka often tells stories about the search for meaning and the process of navigating the branching possibilities of our experience in and understanding of the world. Moreover, perhaps our arrival at interpretive conclusions participates in that process and affirms the inescapability of attempting to read the world in an empowered way, even if we are always missing the point. That issue marks a critical intersection of the writing of Kafka, the writing *about* Kafka, and, connecting back to the framework of this particular study, the writing of Blanchot. Kafka emerges as one of the central figures in Blanchot's critical texts, and the way that Blanchot deals with Kafka's writing reflects the various difficulties that arise when responding to his work. In *The Space of Literature*, Blanchot largely focuses on Kafka's *Diaries* as a means of discussing the experience of writing and the disappearance of the writer in this solitary experience. Before exploring the question of the writer's disappearance, and in particular the way that this disappearance takes shape in Kafka's story "The Burrow," it is necessary to address issues of reading and interpretation that arise when suggesting metaliterary connections between Kafka's narrator and the figure of the writer.

In Benjamin's essay "Some Reflections on Kafka," he notes the way critics have heavily focused on Kafka's personal writings as a means for interpreting his fictions—"to the neglect of his real works."[22] Benjamin's comments point to the tendency to search for and supposedly locate the "key" to Kafka's narratives, thereby reducing the labyrinthine nature of the texts to a single, navigable path. He tells us that "both the psychoanalytical and theological interpretations equally miss the central points [of Kafka's works]" and goes on to explore the way that those works evoke a "prehistoric world" that lies underneath, before, and beyond their simultaneously familiar and foreign textual environments (23, 27). In effect, Benjamin argues that efforts to illuminate the meaning of Kafka's narratives through, for example, the Freudian lens of his troubled relationship with his father, defy the relation to the dark and the unknown—a relation that remains central and must be maintained in the experience of Kafka's work. In *Kafka: Toward a Minor Literature*, Deleuze and Guattari proceed in a similar vein, rejecting uniquely content-oriented analyses that drastically miss the proliferating character of the narrative and linguistic processes at play in Kafka's work. They begin their study:

> How can we enter into Kafka's work? This work is a rhizome, a burrow. The castle has multiple entrances whose rules of usage and whose locations aren't very well known. The hotel in *Amerika* has innumerable main doors and side doors that innumerable main guards watch over; it even has entrances and exits without doors. Yet it might seem that the burrow in the story of that name has only one entrance; the most the animal can do is dream of a second entrance that would serve only as surveillance. But this a trap arranged by the animal and by Kafka himself; the whole description of the burrow functions to trick the enemy. We will enter, then, by any point whatsoever; none matters more than another, and no entrance is more privileged even if it seems an impasse, a tight passage, a siphon.[23]

Interestingly, Deleuze and Guattari's anti-interpretive study of Kafka begins with what seems to be a series of metaphors.[24] Kafka's work resembles a burrow, a castle with multiple hidden entrances, a well-guarded hotel with countless doors—comparisons that suggest a metaliterary relationship between the structures found within Kafka's texts and the texts themselves. Yet the comparison undermines the relationship at the same time that it establishes it. If we accept that Kafka's work is a sort of burrow (or castle, or hotel), then we also must accept that we have entered at a single point, no more or less important than any other number of points where we may choose to enter. Kafka's work is indeed a burrow, and in being so, resists our efforts to read it as any one thing in particular, including a burrow. Regardless, Deleuze and Guattari seem to want the reader to experience the work as an animal getting lost in the proliferating passages of an underground world, or as a land surveyor wandering at the margins of the castle.

Benjamin and other critics suggest that Kafka's narratives function as parables, although this categorization often comes with various qualifications that prevent one from coming to easy conclusions about the way that the parabolic form might point to a privileged meaning. As soon as Benjamin identifies Kafka's stories as parables, he adds that "[i]t is their misery and their beauty that they had to become *more* than parables."[25] If a parable signifies by pointing away from itself, then, traditionally speaking, its message depends upon the understanding of where the parable points. While Kafka's narratives often take the form of parable, they emphasize the pointing away itself and resist attempts to locate the other side of this operation. Theodor Adorno clarifies this idea in "Notes on Kafka":

> Walter Benjamin rightly defined [Kafka's prose] as parable. It expresses itself not through expression but by its repudiation, by breaking off. It is a parabolic system the key to which has been stolen; yet any effort to make this fact itself the key is bound to go astray by confounding the abstract thesis of Kafka's work, the obscurity of the existent, with its substance. Each sentence says "interpret me," and none will permit it.[26]

Again, Adorno emphasizes the danger of interpreting Kafka's work, at the same time that the work demands interpretation—especially when considering it as parable. Looking at Kafka's narratives as parables brings attention to the paradox of our task as readers: we are asked to "go beyond" and then met with the refusal of a sealed door. Kafka's texts send us away and then do it again wherever we arrive, pressing us to look elsewhere.

Kafka's own narrative reflection on the subject, "On Parables," provides an especially interesting look at the telling and understanding of parables. The text begins:

> Many complain that the words of the wise are always merely parables and of no use in daily life, which is the only life we have. When the sage says: "Go over," he does not mean that we should cross to some actual place, which we could do anyhow if the labor were worth it; he means some fabulous yonder, something unknown to us, something that he cannot designate more precisely either, and therefore cannot help us here in the very least.[27]

Those who labor in the world, working to make everything available to comprehension, have no use for parables, which ask us to leave the world of light and understanding for another, much less locatable and graspable sort of space—one where we can't ever really arrive and that we can only experience in its turning away. In this way, the sage, though defined as wise, does not impart wisdom or truth. In response to such a complaint about the uselessness of parables, a man counters: "If you only followed the parables, you yourselves would become parables and with that rid of all your daily cares" (457). Another responds, "I bet that is also a parable," and we find ourselves immersed in a series of parables—a parable within a parable about parables—each asking us to "go over" apparently in order to determine the value of going over (457). At the end of the brief text (or parable), we learn that the second man, in figuring out that the first man's statement is itself a parable, has "won" in reality but lost in parable. It would seem that his logical, singular understanding of the first man's comment provides an answer of sorts, identifying and categorizing it as parable; at the same time, he is functioning according to the demands of reality, rather than to those of parable, which results in his loss. Of course, my reading brings me dangerously close to the trap that ensnares the second man, which I believe is part of the dynamic of reading suggested by Kafka (and later developed by Blanchot). The demand of "going over" in search of meaning often brings us to a point where we risk failing the parable—by grasping it and thereby missing it completely. This risk threatens every reading—certainly one which considers "The Burrow" as a sort of parable of the writer's disappearance in the process of his never-ending work—but also allows us to respond to the demand of the text, perhaps precisely in experiencing the limitations of our reading.

Turning now to Blanchot in our meandering approach to "The Burrow," we shift our attention to the process of writing. In "The Essential Solitude," Blanchot explains that the act of journaling, in the case of a writer, becomes a desperate attempt to ground oneself in the world of everyday activities. Since the writer senses his or her own disappearance when responding to the demand of literature, it might make sense that he or she would seek to reappear in the world, where things can seemingly be measured in time and tasks. The writer runs the risk of losing the ability to say "I" when at work, but, in the journal, writing turns from the demand of literature and appears to establish a relationship with possibility—the possibility to express oneself and the truth of the world. Blanchot calls the journal a "memorial" where the writer remembers what has been lost or has disappeared in the practice of writing; he notes the irony that "the tool he uses in order to recollect himself is, strangely, the very element of forgetfulness: writing" (*SL* 29). And I would add that perhaps the journal is a memorial not only to the writer, but also to a type of language that would make things appear rather than disappear. The writer's choice of tool suggests a desire to transform the tool into something useful and empowering, and momentarily to justify the sacrifice of one's life to writing and to the risk it entails. Of course, this reasoning is problematic, as is the belief that the writer can say "I" in the journal any more definitively than he or she can in a literary work. Regardless, Blanchot brings our attention to the way that the writer's journal expresses his or her struggle with the essential solitude imposed by the work, and often results in a difficult relationship with everyday life, where the writer experiences a sort of double exclusion—from both the work and the world.

In *The Space of Literature*, Blanchot spends much more time discussing Kafka's *Diaries* than he does any particular story or novel. Kafka's *Diaries* allow Blanchot to explore the experience of writing as it is documented throughout Kafka's journaling—both in the sense that the *Diaries* include fragments of stories and show us something of the writing process, and in the sense that they demonstrate Kafka's inability to find a place in the world or in his work. Blanchot writes in a footnote, "His is thus not only a 'Journal' as we understand this genre today, but the very movement of the experience of writing, very close to its beginning and in the essential sense which Kafka was led to give this term" (57). On the one hand, Blanchot is interested in Kafka's *Diaries* because they do indeed demonstrate the general concern of journaling—to keep track of and establish one's place in everyday life. And, on the other, Blanchot contends that Kafka's journaling reveals much more than a desire to write as if he weren't writing (to write without risking disappearance). Kafka writes about his job, his family, and his plans for marriage, often with a marked sense of despair over his inability to find contentment or fulfillment in any of these things. But, perhaps more importantly, it seems that writing both creates and responds to that despair and lack of fulfillment in the world. When discussing the demand of the work, Blanchot writes:

[. . .] [T]he artist who willingly exposes himself to the risks of the experience which is his does not feel free of the world, but, rather, deprived of it; he does not feel that he is master of himself, but rather that he is absent from himself and exposed to demands which, casting him out of life and of living, open him to that moment at which he cannot do anything and is no longer himself. (53)

Blanchot seems to respond here to the idea that art liberates the artist or writer from the concerns of the world and takes him or her to some higher realm of ideas and truth. Rather, Blanchot suggests, the writer experiences his or her exclusion from the world and from life, at the same time that the space of the work offers no solace and no sense of place that would counter such a profound exclusion. The writer begins to disappear from the world, perhaps coming back to it from time to time in order to try to re-establish a connection, a sense of existence. But these moments of "coming back" point to the demand of the work, which threatens to expose the writer to the loss and disappearance of himself or herself in both the world and the work.

Readers of Kafka necessarily note the difficulty he had in finishing his works. Max Brod and some of Kafka's translators sometimes addressed this "problem" by making editorial decisions about what to include, what not to include, and how to piece the fragments together. Kafka himself discusses this issue in his *Diaries*, as he laments, "I can't write any more. I've come up against the last boundary, before which I shall in all likelihood again sit down for years, and then in all likelihood begin another story all over again that will again remain unfinished. This fate pursues me."[28] And, indeed, we actually see this take place in the *Diaries*, with several lines here and there that appear to be pieces of narrative, beginnings of stories. In Jorge Luis Borges's preface to his translation of *The Metamorphosis*, he suggests that Kafka's unfinished texts reflect the subject matter of the work: "The pathos of these inconclusive novels arises precisely from the infinite number of obstacles that detain and detain again his identical heroes. Franz Kafka didn't finish them because the primordial issue was that they were unending" (11).[29] This makes sense, perhaps especially when reading works such as *The Castle* and *The Trial*, and the question becomes how to construe what appears to be a relationship between the task of writing and the heroes who inhabit the texts. Blanchot would certainly hesitate to solidify or affirm this relationship by reading the heroes as a definitive representation of Kafka himself, or the writer in general. But he does not deny the relationship; rather, he poses it as a question:

> To what extent was Kafka aware of the analogy between this move outside truth [of both Josef K. and K.] and the movement by which the work tends toward its origin—toward that center

which in the only place the work can be achieved, in the search for which it is realized and which, once reached, makes the work impossible? To what extent did he connect the ordeal of his heroes with the way in which he himself, through art, was trying to make his way toward the work and, through the work, toward something true? (*SL* 81)

Blanchot presents the relationship between the plight of the heroes and the experience of writing as a question that remains open. Whether Kafka was "aware" or not is perhaps beside the point. We do get the sense, though, that Kafka tells (and enacts) a similar story in a variety of ways over the course of his life, whether in his narratives or his *Diaries*, and that it is possible to see parallels and repetitions without imposing a definitive allegorical reading upon the text.[30] Blanchot continues:

> This much at least is strikingly evident: the fault which he punished in K. is also the one with which the artist reproaches himself. Impatience is this fault. It wants to hurry the story toward its dénouement before the story has developed in all its directions, exhausted the measure of time which is in it, lifted the indefinite to a true totality where every inauthentic movement, every partially false image can be transformed into an unshakable certitude. (81)

K. wants to force himself into the castle, to leap to the end in order to avoid or surpass the wandering and unknowingness of the approach. Yet K. fails to arrive at the end, at the source, at something that would provide and guarantee the truth and meaning of his experience. For Blanchot, the *Diaries* demonstrate the same desire, the same struggle. On some level, Kafka's heroes live out the experience of writing and echo what we read about this experience in the *Diaries*. Blanchot refers to Kafka's *Diaries* in order to trace the demand of the work in the reflections and fragments recorded by Kafka during his life. And turning to the fictions allows us to explore the way that they, too, reflect the demand of the work. With this in mind, I would like to approach "The Burrow," as it tells not only a story of endless wandering, but also, and in keeping with the theme at play in this study, one of profound solitude. Interestingly, the first-person narrative emerges as a sort of journaling, as we read a carefully documented account of the narrator's day-to-day construction of his burrow. The narrator's experience, in all its darkness, paradoxically sheds light upon the risk of disappearance that he confronts, as one who responds to the demand of the work.

The narrator of "The Burrow" begins his story with the triumphant statement: "I have completed the construction of my burrow and it seems to be successful."[31] The story begins by announcing its completion, presenting itself as a (seemingly) successful and finished product. Clearly, this assertion becomes less and less valid as the reader turns the pages of a text that exposes the narrator's inability to find satisfaction, success, or an end in his process of construction. As the narrator obsessively tinkers with the structure of his burrow, we begin to see that this space is anything but finished. He digs new passages, continually moves his storage from place to place, contemplates various structural changes that would improve upon the weaknesses of the burrow, methodically observes the space from the outside and within, theorizes possible dangers, and agonizes over the insurmountable problems of his construction. In this way, the advancement of the narrative, in its literal and figurative relation to the ongoing project of the burrow's construction, necessarily implies a contradiction of its origin, or first sentence. The narrative continually folds back upon its initiation, upsetting any sense of linear progression from the outset. The original German title of Kafka's text is "Der Bau"—the German term for "construction." The English translation loses the ambiguity of the original title, as we often think of construction in positive terms, rather than the underground digging of a negative space. In *Franz Kafka: Geometrician of Metaphor*, Henry Sussman notes, "This terminology is inherently ironic, as the construction consists in hollowing, not protrusion, in the addition of complication, not assertion, in the expansion of darkness, not illumination. The construction is already deconstruction to the same extent that it has been constructed."[32] Moreover, the presentation of the story as that which is in excess of the end recalls Hegel's notion of the end of art and Blanchot's appropriation of that notion to discuss the way that writing represents a movement beyond constructive negativity towards a space of disappearance.[33] In Kafka's text, the narrator creates a negative space through his underground labor, and the actual narrative begins at the point when productivity and labor give way to the lingering sense of what has not been (and cannot be) accomplished or mastered.

While the tone of the narrative reflects the pride of the narrator in the beginning of "The Burrow," it does not take long for questions and insecurities to arise, which quickly overtake any sense of accomplishment that the narrator enjoys. Even though the burrow "is secured as safely as anything in this world can be secured," the narrator recognizes that anyone or anything could potentially discover the entrance, even by accident, which would represent an immediate threat ("BW" 325). He imagines other burrowers seeking to raid his stores, or to feed themselves upon his own flesh, and worries that he could get caught unaware in one of the central sections of his home without a way to escape. Most of the narrator's concerns seem more or less reasonable, but he also soon begins to lose himself to paranoid thinking at times: "[. . .] and my enemies are countless; it could well happen that in flying from one enemy I might run into the jaws of another. Anything might happen!" (326). The narrator clearly becomes obsessed with the potential dangers of his burrow, and his fear drives both the narrative and the continual dismantling and rearranging of his life's work. After moments of frenzy and worrying, he sometimes finds his way back to a sense of satisfaction in his construction (especially earlier in the text), but always manages to return again to the various weaknesses he perceives and imagines new threats that demand his attention. This first aspect of Kafka's depiction of the creative process seems to suggest the impossibility of arriving at a point where one feels finished, secure, and content with the work. Furthermore, the lack of satisfaction and inability to complete the work propel the work forward, beyond the point of "creativity" and towards a space where one experiences the undoing of the work. The maker of the work ultimately loses him or herself in the process of this undoing, fully and perhaps obsessively engaging in a movement that slips beyond his or her grasp.

In addition to the potential enemies that might tunnel their way into the burrow, the narrator tells us of other beasts that might lie beneath his home, threatening him from the depths of the earth. The description of this fear shows that the narrator not only worries about the tangible dangers he faces, but also about those with a more mythic existence:

There are also enemies in the bowels of the earth. I have never seen them, but legend tells of them and I firmly believe in them. They are creatures of the inner earth; not even legend can describe them. Their very victims can scarcely have seen them; they come, you hear the scratching of their claws just under you in the ground, which is their element, and already you are lost. Here it is of no avail to console yourself with the thought that you are in your own house; far rather you are in theirs. (326)

At this point in the text, the narrator simply mentions the possibility that he might someday confront these legendary underground enemies, but the possibility remains at the level of the imaginary. We will see later in the narrative that the approach of a beast from the ungraspable darkness becomes the narrator's central concern and demonstrates his own movement towards that darkness. This is the first inkling of the narrator's growing awareness of his paradoxical exclusion from his "own house." In the first half of the text, though, the narrator's thinking and behavior remains largely practical and rational as he still clings to the possibility of managing his burrow. Despite his worries, he imagines himself to be maker and master of the burrow, perhaps sensing the potential of his disappearance but actively laboring to perfect his creation. He relishes in the experience of silence and stillness that the burrow affords: "There I sleep the sweet sleep of tranquility, of satisfied desire, of achieved ambition; for I possess a house" (327).

The burrow consists of a vast series of tunnels that have near their center a large room called the Castle Keep. The narrator describes:

In the Castle Keep I assemble my stores; everything over and above my daily wants that I capture inside the burrow, and everything I bring back with me from my hunting expeditions outside, I pile up here. The place is so spacious that food for half a year scarcely fills it. Consequently I can divide up my stores, walk about among them, play with them, enjoy their plenty and their various smells, and reckon up exactly how much they represent. (328)

The stores of the Castle Keep represent the excess of the narrator's productive hunting activities. The decaying animal carcasses are not needed for the subsistence of the narrator, and therefore do not fulfill any immediate purpose. We see that the narrator plays with them, admires them, smells them, quantifies them, and divides them up within the central space of the burrow; for the most part, he refrains from eating the carcasses, unless overtaken by a moment of gluttony. It is within the Castle Keep that the narrator can indulge in this sort of excessive pleasure, for the moment not worrying about the immediate concerns for survival that dominate the rest of the narrative. The playful and enjoyable activity with the stores of the burrow reflects the narrator's pride in his hunting accomplishments, at the same time that it affirms the secure space of the Castle Keep—a space that is certainly fit for survival, considering its size and valuable contents. Thus we see a connection between the narrator's relatively carefree behavior and the security promised by the space within which he is able momentarily to put his worries aside. Yet there comes a time when the narrator decides that the stores of his burrow represent not only abundance, but also danger.

As the narrator reflects back upon the process of constructing the Castle Keep, he explains that it sometimes overwhelmed him and certainly took much physical and mental perseverance over the course of the project.

> Several times, on the despair brought on by physical exhaustion, I was on the point of giving up the whole business, flung myself down panting and cursed the burrow, dragged myself outside and left the place lying open to all the world. I could afford to do that, for I had no longer any wish to return to it, until at last, after four hours or days, back I went repentantly, and when I saw that the burrow was unharmed I could almost have raised a hymn of thanksgiving, and in sincere gladness of heart started on the work anew. (328)

We see the struggle of the artist at work here, abandoning the project out of a sense that his continual toil does not lead to anything worthwhile. Yet the work calls him back, and the artist regrets his hasty decision with a renewed hope in the potential of his creative abilities—paradoxically re-engaging in a process that subverts the ability to do anything. This cycle of abandonment and return recalls Blanchot's description of the writer who seems to start over and over again, as if from the same place, hoping to accomplish what eluded him before. It demonstrates "the necessity, which apparently determines his efforts, that he always come back to the same point, pass again over the same paths, persevere in starting over what for him never starts [. . .]" (*SL* 24). The act of stopping, of giving up, actually represents the writer's (and the narrator's) ability, while the resumption of the work opens a space of inability where the writer necessarily disappears. In that space, he no longer has the power to act, accomplish, or say "I," thus relinquishing the ability to appear and exist in the world. This issue is demonstrated in very literal ways in "The Burrow," as the narrator's re-engagement in his work completely sequesters him from the outside world; the narrator chooses darkness, and, in doing so, sacrifices the ability to choose, and even to exist in, the light of day.

After finishing the Castle Keep, the narrator at first feels extremely pleased with the central storage space, but he begins to worry that it is dangerous to invest everything in a single room. At this point the narrator's once playful activity with his abundant stores becomes serious and even desperate, exposing the inherent and uncontrollable "free play" within the burrow's structure. In the seemingly closed, finite space of the burrow, the narrator can disperse and re-disperse the contents in any way he chooses; his efforts to create a sense of security by moving the stores from the Castle Keep to other rooms ultimately fail to provide a sense of safety or comfort. Furthermore, in an attempt to secure the burrow by dispersing its goods, the narrator decentralizes the space and opens the burrow up to a much less comforting and containable playfulness that arises with the shifting of the burrow's contents.[34] After he disperses his stores, the narrator almost immediately brings them back to the central Castle Keep, returning to the initial idea of keeping his goods together. Finally, he concludes:

> The idea of dividing up my stores is of course a good one, but only if one had several rooms similar to my Castle Keep. Several such rooms! Indeed! [...] But I will admit that that is a fault in my burrow; it is always a fault to have only one copy of anything. [...] I felt too feeble for the enormous labor it would involve, I felt too feeble even to admit to myself the necessity for that labor. (278-279)

The narrator struggles with the thought of not having a central location for the contents of his burrow; while he admits the advantages of having several storage rooms, the act of decentralizing his burrow seems both out of reach and undesirable. Not only would it involve a great amount of labor, but also, making copies of the Castle Keep would certainly devalue the purpose and privileged place of the original Castle Keep. While the narrator eventually decides to return the carcasses to the Castle Keep (making the activity of transporting them worthless, unproductive labor), the sense of mobility and changeability that arises from this work reveals a haunting instability in regards to the space of the burrow. We might infer that the narrator returns the burrow's contents to the Castle Keep in order to reaffirm its centrality and meaningfulness. Unfortunately, the deliberate effort to establish and re-establish centrality points to the desire to provide a center for that which is revealed to have none. Again, the narrator finds himself struggling to act as an empowered presence in his work, since the work clearly resists those efforts and calls the narrator's role in the work into question.

Interesting comparisons can be made to some of Kafka's other narratives, where the hero has a complicated relation with a central space or Law—one that would seem to promise some sort of meaning or stability and would thereby structure the hero's advancement towards a final goal. In his essay "Parable as Paradox in Kafka's Stories," Alwin Baum refers to the *Gesetzbuch* that the Kafkan hero seeks—"a code of codes" that would make sense of the hero's experiences and provide a means for fulfilling his task.[35] The heroes wander marginally, never coming into contact with the central Law of the environment they inhabit, but ceaselessly chasing after it. Baum notes, "The seriousness with which Kafka's heroes pursue the quest for the *Gesetzbuch* threatens, however, to obscure the irony embedded in the parable of the quest itself" (152). He then provides the example of Josef K.'s discovery of the Examining Magistrate's notebook in *The Trial*, which ends up merely containing a seemingly random "indecent picture" of a man and a woman on a couch. Significantly, the heroes who do happen upon a central space or book of some sort ultimately confront the absence of an organizing principle or universal Law; in other words, the *Gesetzbook* reveals itself as fraudulent. In "The Burrow," the narrator does indeed have a center to his structure— one he created himself, packing the walls with the force of his head—but that center fails to provide stability and ultimately exposes the vulnerability of the burrow. The Castle Keep could eventually become the cause of the narrator's literal disappearance, as it invites scavenging enemies into the burrow. And, beyond that possibility, its shortcomings and groundlessness engage the narrator in a work that has no conclusion and confronts him with his inability to do anything in the space of the burrow, regardless of the blood that trickles from his head while attempting to solidify the walls.

The narrator explains that his construction began with the maze-like structure that now lies at the outer limit of the burrow. Since he was merely commencing the project that eventually became the complicated and expansive structure he now claims to have finished, the narrator clearly had less at stake at this early point in his construction. He reflects:

> [. . .] I began, half in play, at that corner, and so my first joy in labor found riotous satisfaction there in a labyrinthine burrow which at the time seemed to me the crown of all burrows,

but which I judge today, perhaps with more justice, to be too much of an idle *tour de force*, not really worthy of the rest of the burrow, and though perhaps theoretically brilliant—here is my main entrance, I said in those days, ironically addressing my invisible enemies and seeing them all already caught and stifled in the outer labyrinth—is in reality a flimsy piece of jugglery that would hardly withstand a serious attack or the struggles of an enemy fighting for his life. (331)

In this retrospective look at the burrow's initiation, we notice the clearly contrasting attitude that the narrator had towards his construction. He appears to have lacked the oppressive expectations and anxiety that drive his current activities in the burrow—at this earlier time digging "half in play" and experiencing "riotous satisfaction" (331). Such vocabulary suggests that this activity did not simply seek to meet practical demands; rather, the burrower created a labyrinth that promised artfully to deceive and frustrate any being that enters its winding paths. The narrator clearly took pride in his work; but once the burrow expanded beyond this game-like labyrinth in order to serve as a secure and carefully meditated home, the same qualities that once brought him joy now become the object of his critique. The narrator refers to the outer labyrinth as a "*tour de force*"—a notable expression that evokes artistic achievement—but also negatively qualifies this expression with the adjective "idle" (331). In addition, he remembers dramatizing heroic encounters with his enemies who fall victim to the trap, but then follows the memory of this past theatricality with the present belief that this section of his burrow is "a flimsy piece of jugglery" (331). The language in this passage points to the distinction that the narrator makes between playful, idle, even artistic, behavior and practical, useful work. The narrator associates the margins of the burrow with a younger, more naïve self who has left a lasting defect on what could otherwise be an impressive, masterful structure. We may also note that the margins only become marginal once progressive digging and structuration create a centered space. In this way, the outer edges of the burrow paradoxically represent both origin and marginality, which necessarily puts into question the stability of the burrow's center as the site of organization and meaning.

The narrator's negative, anxious attitude towards the outer labyrinth of his burrow suggests skepticism about what seems to represent a more playful, even artistic, realm. The labyrinth has at its outer limit two entrances, one of which is covered with a mossy layer to disguise it. The other entrance lies "at a distance of some thousand paces" from the moss covering and actually does not penetrate the burrow—it is a ruse (325). Sussman describes the two entrances, beginning with the moss-covered hole:

> It incorporates both a stratum of apparently solid and "natural" reality and the convolutions of its internal logic, calculated to befuddle possible intruders. The construction resists penetration. One of its doubled openings is self-evident. This is the one, however, leading nowhere. The only available access is by way of fiction, through the moss camouflage that is the entrance's only protection.[36]

What exactly does Sussman mean by "fiction" here? He contrasts it with that which is self-evident and then associates it with disguise and deception. Paradoxically, the seemingly self-evident entrance to the burrow leads nowhere because it is a ruse, while the deceptive, "fictional" entrance provides a way in—even if one is met with the complete darkness of an underground labyrinth. The burrow resists penetration both by the trickery of its entrances and by its subsequent windings, suggesting that fiction (if we accept Sussman's designation) does not welcome, but, rather, wards off intruders. In addition, anyone entering the space of the burrow must give him or herself over to the darkness, risking his or her own disappearance in this movement away from the light of the outside world.

The narrator strictly avoids the outer labyrinth of his construction during his "customary rounds," trying hard to forget the area he considers to be defective and weak. While the thought of the entrance itself, and the possibility that it might be discovered, is unnerving, the narrator explains that the outer labyrinth "torments [him] most of all" (332). He despises the imperfections of the burrow's margins and feels at his most vulnerable when nearing that space:

> If I merely walk in the direction of the entrance, even though I may be separated by it from several rooms and passages, I find myself sensing an atmosphere of great danger, actually as if my hair were growing thin and in a moment might fly off and leave me bare and shivering, exposed to the howls of my enemies. (332)

The narrator feels extreme fear when nearing the labyrinth —not because he senses entrapment or suffocation within its thin, winding passages, but rather because he fears complete exposure in this realm. Thus, while the margins of the burrow bear a relationship to disguise and enclosure when warding off potential intruders from the outside, they also threaten to expose, or reveal, the narrator in his most undisguised, unprotected, and naked self. As we imagine in the navigation of any kind of labyrinth, the question of perspective arises: movement within a labyrinth and the experience of this movement depend upon whether one is trying to achieve ingress or egress. To an interested animal seeking to penetrate the burrow, the disguised entrance and labyrinthine windings represent deception and entrapment; but for the narrator within the burrow, the maze exposes vulnerability and subverts any attempt at disguise. The defects of the outer labyrinth seem to turn a sort of mirror on the narrator, making him painfully aware of his own imperfections and inability to fix what he has made. The narrator attempts to separate himself from his work where it concerns the labyrinth, at the same time that this separation affirms the relation between his sense of self and his construction. Its defects become his defects and expose his inability to accomplish his work. The narrator's only relief from that torment comes when, he explains, "[. . .] as sometimes happens, I lose myself for a moment in my own maze, and the work of my hands seems to be still doing its best to prove its sufficiency to me, its maker [. . .]" (133). Significantly, the narrator must lose himself in order to experience satisfaction, partially because his getting lost points to the success of the labyrinth; furthermore, getting lost allows him to approach the burrow's maze from the perspective not of its maker, but its wanderer. At a figurative level, that light, careless wandering recalls Blanchot's characterization of the reader, who winds through the passages of a text without him or herself being at stake.

From time to time, the narrator decides to leave his burrow in order to do some hunting and also to surveil his burrow from the outside. An excursion represents a great risk to the narrator, who thinks to himself, "Your house is protected and self-sufficient. You live in peace, warm, well nourished, master, sole master of all your manifold passages and rooms, and all this you are prepared—not to give up, of course—but to risk it, so to speak" (333). The idealistic musings of the narrator upon his departure contradict the preceding litany of worries about his inability to be master of his home and to construct a space that is truly protected. Still, the narrator feels hesitant to leave, up until the moment that he races through the moss covering, attempting to go undetected out of his entrance. Once outside, he confesses, "Yet I am not really free" (333). Despite the fact that the narrator now has free range in the woods to hunt and is no longer enclosed within the confines of the burrow, he remains unable to stop obsessing about his home. Rather than enjoying the freedom of the outside world, the narrator finds himself back at the entrance of the burrow, hiding in a place from which he can observe the happenings directly outside of his underground structure. At first, as is his pattern, the narrator takes satisfaction in what he observes and feels empowered by his position of surveillance:

> At such times it is as if I were not so much looking at my house as at myself sleeping, and had the joy of being in a profound slumber and simultaneously of keeping vigilant guard over myself. I am privileged, as it were, not only to dream about the specters of the night in all the helplessness and blind trust of sleep, but also at the same time to confront in actuality with the calm judgment of the fully awake. And strangely enough I discover that my situation is not so bad as I had often thought, and will probably think again when I return to my house. (334)

We see in this passage that the narrator identifies himself with his work, observing it as if he were observing himself from the outside. The observing "self" camped outside of the burrow feels a sense of power, an ability to keep guard over the self that sleeps in the dark. The narrator's excursion allows him to appear and to exist in the outside world, defined by his ability to act in "calm judgment." His rational conclusions alleviate the anxieties that had been building, even if he recognizes the probability that the anxieties will re-emerge once he returns to his burrow. Regardless, we see the way that the narrator's sense of being is closely intertwined with his work, which suggests that the ultimate impossibility of the work will have grave implications for his own possibility—to act, to manage, to exist.

Even though the narrator's initial observations of the burrow from the outside bring him comfort, he begins to question the value of his findings; he realizes that he cannot judge the protective qualities of his construction when it is not engaged in the act of protecting. After all, when the narrator is outside, the burrow no longer has anything to protect (with the exception, perhaps, of the stores) and certainly does not invite intrusion to the same extent as it does when the narrator could be trapped inside. He laments:

> What does this protection that I am looking at here from the outside amount to after all? Dare I estimate the danger which I run inside the burrow from observations which I make from outside? Can my enemies, to begin with, have any proper awareness of me if I am not in my burrow? (335)

The narrator cannot sufficiently observe the burrow from the outside, nor can he observe the outside from the inside of the burrow. This situation makes it impossible for the narrator to judge his work; no amount of careful observation will lead him to a definitive conclusion about the sufficiency of his construction.

The work therefore holds the maker at an unsurpassable distance from what he has created, both inside and out. Despite the artist's full investment in his work, and the entanglement of the work with his sense of being, the work excludes him. After the realization of his powerlessness, the narrator admits, "No, I do not watch over my sleep, as I imagined; rather, it is I who sleep, while the destroyer watches" (335). It seems that despite the narrator's attempts to claim the roles of both masterful subject of the gaze and the sleeping, helpless object of observation, he eventually recognizes that he is a part of the dark, even though he comes out into the light of day in an attempt to re-assert himself in the world.

The narrator briefly entertains the possibility of joining forces with a "confidant" who would guard the burrow once the narrator descends, taking note of any animals that might pose a threat. He concludes, though, that "to trust someone outside the burrow when you are inside the burrow, that is, in a different world, that, it seems to me, is impossible" (338). The narrator feels so cut off from the outside that he sees himself as living in a "different world"—one that is impossibly distant from the light of day. This situation emphasizes the narrator's complete solitude. While he does indeed venture out of the burrow into the world, he remains, in fact, unable to leave it, and seems to spend most of his time obsessively observing the space near the entrance. The narrator perceives all other animals as enemies and quickly rejects the notion that he could acquire a confidant to help protect his burrow. He adds that "to let anyone freely into my burrow, would be exquisitely painful for me," which assures that he can and will descend into his work alone (338). Once he decides to do so, the next problem becomes the descent itself—how can he re-enter the burrow without drawing dangerous attention to the entrance? The narrator agonizes over this question, especially when "confronted by that entrance over there which now literally locks and bars itself against [him], the builder and possessor" (340). The narrator's exclusion from his work becomes even more apparent, as it now resists his entry and therefore puts into question his sovereignty over the construction that he sacrificed himself to create. The space of the burrow rejects the narrator's notion of mastery and possession, and his step outside of the burrow reveals the powerlessness of his role in the movement of the work. In *The Space of Literature*, Blanchot makes a comment about the writer that illuminates the narrator's struggle at this point in the narrative: "Every writer, every artist is acquainted with the moment at which he is cast out and apparently excluded by the work in progress. The work holds him off, the circle in which he no longer has access to himself has closed, yet he is enclosed therein because the work, unfinished, will not let him go" (53). Like the writer in this passage, the narrator of "The Burrow" experiences his exclusion from the work, despite the sense that he is simultaneously enclosed within the space of the work, which remains open and unfinished. The work dismisses him at the same time that it hangs on, demanding the narrator's re-entry into its space while promising an even darker, more drastic exclusion. The work's affirmation comes about by way of the artist's exclusion, thereby necessitating his sacrifice and disappearance in the movement towards an ultimate refusal.

Eventually, the narrator risks his enemies' discovery of the entrance to his burrow by returning to his home—uncharacteristically with no effort to deceive or disguise, as his sense of defeat makes such strategizing seem pointless.

And then, too exhausted to be any longer capable of thought, my head hanging, my legs trembling with fatigue, half asleep, feeling my way rather than walking, I approach the entrance, slowly raise the moss covering, slowly descend, leaving the door open in my distraction for a needlessly long time, and presently remember my omission, and get out again to make it good [. . .]. Only in this state, and in this state alone can I achieve my descent. (341)

The narrator's re-entry into the burrow lacks the certainty of a decision or an action; he characterizes his return as exhausted, trembling, and half asleep, and he is clearly beaten by the realization of his own powerlessness to overcome the risks of the situation. He no longer has the energy to care, exposing his burrow and accepting its vulnerability as inevitable. Interestingly, the narrator recognizes that his entry into the burrow demands that he relinquish any sense of mastery, giving himself over to the space in a state of helplessness and passivity. Despite the defeated descent, the narrator soon feels reinvigorated, elated by his reunion with his burrow. He explains, "[. . .] I have left the upper world and am in my burrow, and I feel its effects at once. It is a new world, endowing me with new powers, and what I felt as fatigue up there is no longer that down here" (341). Interestingly, the narrator does not pick up where he left off when leaving the burrow, but rather seems to return to the beginning—a time of hope and energy, and a belief in his empowerment now that he has left the anxieties of the upper world. Of course, going back to the narrator's state before he left the burrow, we recall the intense sense of anxiety that plagued him at that time as well. But the narrator must forget in order to re-engage in the process of the work. His language returns to one of productivity and labor as he works at pulling his spoils through the thin passages of the burrow towards the Castle Keep, and he celebrates the "endless time" he has to complete his tasks—"for everything I do there is good and important and satisfies me somehow" (342). The narrator's comments likely strike the reader as ironic, for we do not forget the lack of satisfaction experienced by the narrator before his excursion, nor do we likely miss the less positive implications of the "endless time" that characterizes the narrator's work. In her essay "More Remote Than the Abyss," Laura Quinney remarks the way that the narrator "addresse[s] the burrow with the passion and devotion of an erotic love" when he revels in the happiness of his reunion with the burrow.[37] The narrator exclaims, "What do I care for danger now that I am with you? You belong to me, I to you, we are united: What can harm us? [. . .] And with its silence and emptiness the burrow answers me, confirming my words" ("BW" 342). As Quinney suggests, the narrator takes the burrow's silence as a sign that they are one, foreshadowing the significance of the whistling that disrupts his euphoric return to his home.

Once the narrator hears the "almost inaudible whistling noise" faintly traveling the passages of his burrow, the rest of his narrative is dedicated to the investigation of that noise and the eventual acceptance that it exceeds his ability to do anything about it (343). The investigations begin lightly, as the narrator hypothesizes that familiar, unthreatening, small burrowers have taken some liberties during his excursion to the outer world, not having to fear his presence. The noise eventually becomes nearly ubiquitous and inescapable, resounding the loudest in the Castle Keep, whose "murmurous silence" the narrator can no longer hear (347). In order to discover the cause of the noise, the narrator begins to dismantle his burrow, sacrificing his carefully constructed passages in his obsessive search. He realizes, "[. . .] I merely disfigure the walls of my burrow, scratching hastily here and there without taking time to fill up the holes again; at many places there are heaps of earth which block my way and my view" (348). The narrator becomes so involved with finding the cause of the noise that, in some ways, he becomes the most dangerous threat to the burrow. Uncharacteristically, the narrator acts recklessly, desperate to silence the noise and to restore his burrow to an ideal state of peace that it probably never had. After considerable effort, the narrator arrives at the impossibility of discovering the source of the noise, or, at the least, decides to accept defeat. He reveals, "I have had enough of discoveries; I let everything slide; I would be quite content if I could only still the conflict going on within me" (352). Here, the narrator shifts the attention from his conflict with the noise to the conflict within himself—perhaps suggesting that his inner conflict represents the most threatening, impossible-to-silence noise of all. Since, as we saw before, the silence of the burrow allows the narrator to feel a sense of unity with his work, the noise indicates separation, exclusion, and disharmony. Quinney describes it as "the sign of [the narrator's] estrangement from its own production, investment, and self."[38]

At the point when the narrator gives up his investigations, he becomes a much more passive figure, no longer under the impression that he can manage the space of his work. He also turns from the rational and empirical modes of thinking that characterize his plans to discover the origin of the noise and opens himself to more mythical possibilities. In his failure to find a rational explanation, the narrator returns to the legend of a beast that lives in the unreachable depths of the earth and imagines that the beast will eventually penetrate the burrow. He admits that his "imagination will not rest" and claims that a lack of evidence supporting the existence of the beast simply demonstrates that it is "beyond all one's powers of conception" (353). In a significant shift in perspective, the narrator confronts the limits of his mind and ability to reduce the noise to a rational explanation. Not only does the narrator's perspective change, but he also becomes passive in his daily activity, giving up the frenzied digging and accepting the fact that such activity will not lead him to the noise. He explains, "I have reached the stage where I no longer wish to have certainty. In the Castle Keep I choose a lovely piece of flayed red flesh and creep with it into one of the heaps of earth; there I shall have silence at least, such silence, at any rate, as still can be said to exist here" (319). Interestingly, the noise sounds the loudest in the Castle Keep, and the narrator ultimately turns to the margins of his burrow to find peace and silence. In other words, the space that once promised security now feels most dangerous, whereas the outer labyrinth no longer represents the negative consequences of childish play and comes to serve as the narrator's escape. The reversal in meanings assigned to each space again points to the narrator's inability to ground his structure in something solid and stable. Once in the outer labyrinth, the narrator continues to assess his situation, reflecting on past decisions and possibilities for the future. He comes to the conclusion that, despite all of his activities, "All remained unchanged," which is both the final sentence of the narrative and the extreme expression of his powerlessness (359).

While Blanchot does not discuss "The Burrow" at length in

any of his critical texts, he offers a few comments in *The Space of Literature* about the implications of the haunting noise in the story. He describes the narrator's underground labors as the descent in the first night, much like Orpheus's artistic ability to open the depths of the underworld in order to retrieve Eurydice. Although the narrator lives in the dark, he remains active and productive, fashioning his burrow in a particular way in order to make it invulnerable. Blanchot writes:

> There you assure yourself of solid defenses against the world above, but leave yourself open to the insecurity of the underneath. You build after day's fashion, but below ground, and what rises sinks, what is erected is swallowed up. The more the burrow seems solidly closed to the outside, the greater the danger that you be closed in with the outside, delivered to the peril without any means of escape. And when every foreign threat seems shut out of this perfectly closed intimacy, then it is intimacy that becomes menacing foreignness. (*SL* 168)

The other side of the narrator's labor descends much deeper, and opens onto a much more threatening outside—one that is infinitely outside but manages to penetrate and to become the intimacy of the burrow. The whistling noise announces the outside, the *other* night, in its infinite absence. When the narrator first hears the noise, he desires to grasp it by discovering its origin and bringing it into his understanding. But the noise exceeds the narrator's actions; his relation to the noise arises out of its refusal to appear and to make itself known. Moreover, the narrator's perception of the noise points to all of the implications of the other night, which include his own alterity—himself as infinitely other, like the noise, only met in its refusal to be grasped. According to Blanchot (who refers to the narrator as "the beast," and thus suggests the relation of the narrator and the noise): "What the beast senses in the distance—that monstrous thing which eternally approaches it and works eternally at coming closer—is itself. And if the beast could ever come into this thing's presence, what it would encounter would be its own absence: itself, but itself become the other, which it would not recognize, which it would not meet" (169). For Blanchot, the narrator's labor—the constructive negativity of digging a burrow—takes him to the limit of his productive abilities. After all, he finishes his burrow at the outset of the narrative. Yet, at that limit, something still murmurs in the distance and haunts the narrator as that which no amount of digging can reach. When the narrator's digging has finished creating a space, the digging persists, only this time not as labor. That infinite and ungraspable surplus points to the narrator's impossible relation with his work and with himself as other.

Earlier in *The Space of Literature*, Blanchot proposes, "The work requires of the writer that he lose everything he might construe as his own "nature," that he lose all character and that, ceasing to be linked to others and to himself by the decision which makes him an "I," he becomes the empty place where impersonal affirmation occurs" (55). The narrator of "The Burrow," whether or not we read this story as a parable of the writing process in particular, demonstrates the solitude and exclusion experienced by a "maker" in relation to his or her work. The narrator disappears into the night, the darkness of his burrow, by way of his productive digging. Out of darkness, he makes his burrow appear as a solid, protective structure, and he thus gives rise to his own appearance as the master of the burrow. But something escapes him, and, in continuing his descent, the narrator begins to confront the loss of the work and the loss of himself: "In solitude he dissolves."[39] The noise persists, indicating the turning away of the work and of the artist as other; and, with nothing else to do, the narrator waits, painfully aware that "all remain[s] unchanged" in the face of his efforts to grasp the abyssal depths of his work and being—depths that precede and exceed both work and being. In this final movement of infinite deferral, the narrator disappears, up against the limit of his (im)possibility.

Chapter 3: Lost in the Labyrinth: Jorge Luis Borges's "The Garden of Forking Paths"

When discussing Jorge Luis Borges in the essay "Literary Infinity: The Aleph," Blanchot implicitly compares the work of Borges to that of Kafka, suggesting that the labyrinth and the desert inspire a similarly errant, endless wandering. Blanchot refers to "the man of the desert and the man of the labyrinth" at the beginning of the essay, encouraging us to see a similar concern at play for both men, as each is "devoted to the error of a journey necessarily a little longer than his life" (*BC* 93). Kafka emerges as the man of the desert throughout Blanchot's numerous essays on his work and life, even if his name never appears in Blanchot's essay on Borges. In *The Space of Literature*, Blanchot writes, "Kafka's wandering does not consist in nearing Canaan, but in nearing the desert, the truth of the desert" (71). We see that a final destination or goal has nothing to do with the sort of wandering that Blanchot evokes here; the truth of the desert would seem to promise only that the wanderer will become more profoundly lost with each step. Similarly, one who navigates a labyrinth might indeed do so with the intent of reaching a particular, privileged point—the center or the exit, for example—but the man of the labyrinth goes nowhere, losing himself in the dizzying, disorienting passages. Blanchot explains that a desert or a labyrinth would seem to represent a finite space with definite boundaries; one can theoretically traverse that space and exit it at will. Yet, in the darkness of the Kafkan desert and the Borgesian labyrinth, a wanderer's steps defy spatial logic and fail to take that person any closer to an exit. Much like Achilles's efforts to catch up to the tortoise in Zeno's paradox—one of Borges's favorite references—the wanderer remains infinitely at a distance from a destination or end point. Blanchot writes:

> The error, the fact of being on the go without ever being able to stop, changes the finite into infinity. And to it these singular changes are added: from the finite, which is still closed, one can always hope to escape, while the infinite vastness is a prison, being without an exit—just as any place absolutely without exit becomes infinite. The place of wandering knows no straight line; one never goes from one point to another in it; one does not leave here to go there; there is no point of departure and no beginning to the walk. (*BC* 94)

Blanchot's language in this passage returns us to the question of powerlessness that he associates with the artistic process; the wanderer remains unable to begin or to finish, as neither act belongs to the sort of space Blanchot describes. He explains, "Before having begun one already begins again," as any effort to advance throws one back to, and arises out of, the beginning, making movement both impossible and infinite (94). That moment of perpetual contestation evokes the "evil infinite"—a notion that Blanchot traces back to Hegel—and also, for Blanchot, touches upon "the truth of literature" (93). Borges's reflections upon the infinite, often arising out of his literal and figurative labyrinths, suggest the withdrawal and disappearance of literature—beyond a structured, ordered space and towards one of ungraspable chaos.

While Blanchot refers to Borges as a man of the labyrinth—an incessant wanderer—some of the labyrinths represented within, and by, Borges's work encourage the reader to proceed on a linear journey, logically linking beginning to end with each piece of the narrative puzzle. As Peter Brooks explains in *Reading for the Plot*, "only the end can determine final meaning," especially when dealing with a mystery or detective story.[40] Once the hermeneut, or detective, has arrived at the final solution, the previously enigmatic and confusing weavings of the narrative leading up to the solution finally achieve order and appear to make perfect, linear sense.[41] In a lecture he gave on the detective story, Borges explained, "In this chaotic era of ours, one thing has humbly maintained the classic virtues: the detective story. For a detective story cannot be understood without a beginning, middle, or end [. . .] it is a safeguarding order in an era of disorder."[42] There is, of course, a certain irony in such a statement: while Borges's fiction often feels extremely well-ordered, sometimes following the general narrative model of the detective story, the creation of that order remains highly self-conscious. Perhaps for this reason, Blanchot proposes, "*Fictions, Artifices* risk being the most honest names that literature can be given" (*BC* 94). In other words, at times the man of the labyrinth might indeed produce a carefully crafted final product, a book—perhaps as a sort of response to his disorderly and wandering experience, and perhaps as a way to *make* something of the world and of his work. Blanchot writes:

> The book is in principle the world for [Borges], and the world is a book. That is what should make him serene about the meaning of the universe, for one can doubt the reason of the universe, but the book that we make—and in particular those cleverly organized books of fiction, like perfectly obscure problems to which perfectly obscure solutions suffice, such as detective novels—we know to be penetrated with intelligence and animated by that power of arrangement that is the mind. (95)

The book becomes the labor of the world—that which employs the power of the mind and of reason to make the universe fit into a graspable, perfectly organized structure. Later in the essay, Blanchot refers to the production of such books as "the energetic labor of negation" (95). He continues, "It is this minus, a sort of thinning, slimming of space, that allows us to go from one point to another according to the fortunate way of the straight line" (95-96). Blanchot sees neatly structured, linear narratives as a form of productive negativity, and opposes that kind of writing to one dedicated to the desert or the labyrinth. Yet, in the work of Borges, the tidy structure self-consciously emerges as fiction, as artifice. Borges uses narrative structure as a form of play, and such play eventually brings our attention to that which exceeds the labor of order and reason, disappearing beyond the limits of what the structure can contain and present. The highly determined, contained structure takes us to the completion of the book, and yet the work remains, disappearing into an infinite, invisible labyrinth that refuses one's ability to navigate. In Borges's work, the figure of the labyrinth sets the stage for the relation between order and disorder, between masterful navigation and powerless wandering.[43]

Borges often mentions the labyrinths that have a simple solution for those who know the secret of their order. As in a detective story, discovering the right key or clue allows one to create a logical narrative path from beginning to end. In "The Garden of Forking Paths," when Yu Tsun gets off the train to find Stephen Albert's house, a group of boys advises him on how to navigate the labyrinthine roads leading to his destination. Yu Tsun reflects, "The boy's advice to turn always to the left reminded me that that was the common way of discovering the central lawn of a certain type of maze."[44] With these directions, Yu Tsun is sure to arrive at Stephen's home without unnecessary meandering or the threat of getting lost. Likewise, in "Ibn-Hakam Al-Bokhari, Murdered in his Labyrinth," the two protagonists also know to turn left at every branching path in order to arrive at its center. Yet, in this story, the narrator evokes an interesting sense of constriction when describing the journey: "Their cautious steps echoed on the stone floor; at every branching, the corridor grew narrower. They felt they were being suffocated by the house—the ceiling was very low. They were forced to walk in single file through the knotted darkness."[45] The labyrinth in this story produces a feeling of claustrophobia, rather than endless possibilities for wandering; the walls of the maze enclose the navigators in a dark, tight, constricting space. It would seem that the lack of choice in this situation begins to feel oppressive, bringing our attention to the way that the easy-to-follow labyrinth traps the characters in an over-determined, inflexible structure. At the same time, such structures comfort us with logic, order, and comprehensibility—attractive traits, even for Borges—and control our navigation of the labyrinth by emphasizing and allowing for the single intent of reaching a destination. Regardless, as ordered as any of Borges's narrative mazes may seem, he rarely (if ever) leaves it at that; easy explanations and solutions often bear the unsettling suggestion of other possibilities and end up feeling limited, even if they take us to our destination.

The labyrinth emerges as a contradictory image in Borges's work, sometimes suggesting the possibility of mastery and linearity, and sometimes pointing to a much less containable and navigable space. Labyrinths differ in their structure and intent, although the general function of the space would seem to consist in confusing, entrapping, and resisting the person who attempts to enter or exit. As Borges himself writes in "The Two Kings and the Two Labyrinths," the most complicated of labyrinths promises to be "so confused and so subtle that the most prudent men would not venture to enter it, and those who did would lose their way."[46] The maker of the labyrinth, much like Daedalus, typically strives to provide a space with an order so difficult to decipher that any who enter shall become lost in its passages. In the specific case of the Minotaur's labyrinth, we know that reaching the center of the construction only presents half of the challenge; retracing one's steps back to the exit, likely with a monster in pursuit, proves to be nearly impossible. As Theseus marks his way with thread, we witness the containment of the labyrinth's forking structure—the thread makes linear (although surely not straight) that which is defined by branching and multiplicity. The Cretan labyrinth does not provide a structure where one could turn left at every crossroads; instead, the ordering of the labyrinth depends upon Theseus's ability to create a single path out of the multiple and to find a certain order in the seemingly chaotic. Of course, in the case of Theseus's journey through the labyrinth, he has a specific task to accomplish, and a destination. In this way, his interest does not lie in the possibility of wandering that the labyrinth offers; rather, he seeks to conquer the structure that threatens to subject him to this dangerous meandering. The labyrinth is a test fit for a hero; as Warren Motte explains in an essay on literary space, it "mobilizes space in order to put the subject to the question, testing his or her resourcefulness."[47] Therefore, if the navigator-hero wanders with purpose and intent, and uses his or her skills to overcome the labyrinth's confusing structure, he or she may reach a given destination, thus defeating the labyrinth.

One of the questions that arise when imagining the labyrinth in this way concerns the imposition of linearity and singularity on a structure that resists those qualities. Clearly, in order to make one's way through the labyrinth—or, figuratively, the book or the world—control and containment of the weaving paths must take place. The deliberate ordering of the labyrinth makes navigating, writing, and reading possible, assuming we want to get somewhere rather than infinitely wandering. But the function of the labyrinth in Borges's work does not always lend itself to the strategic guidance of the thread. As readers, our instincts encourage us to grasp the thread and find our way through the text, but Borges rarely lets us feel satisfied with the choices we have made. Navigating the labyrinth always implies choice—right or left, forward or back— and the thread marks these moments of decision. In *Borges the Labyrinth Maker*, Ana María Barrenechea notes Borges's resistance to choice: "His fantasy proliferates over infinite routes which are divergent, parallel, or intertwined because he weighs the possibility of selecting all destinies and living infinite histories infinitely ramified."[48] As we will see with Ts'ui Pen's novel in "The Garden of Forking Paths," Borges reflects upon the possibility of a narrative structure that subverts the literary act of choosing, and brings our attention to the reductive nature of the choices we necessarily make while writing and reading texts. In mastering the labyrinth with the clever use of thread, do we actually experience the labyrinth, or simply bring its multiple, disorienting paths into the realm of reason and comprehension? It would seem that we make the labyrinth disappear in order to make the most efficient path appear, which ultimately represents "a sort of thinning, slimming of space, that allows us to go from one point to another according to the fortunate way of the straight line" (*BC* 95-6). While Theseus emerges as a hero in Greek mythology, we might imagine, from a Borgesian or Blanchotian perspective, that his empowered navigation keeps him from ever entering the labyrinth.[49]

For Blanchot, the man of the labyrinth is a different sort of figure. And the textual space that Borges fashions in his stories often takes shape through the proliferation of alternate paths, the infinite relation of mirror images, the paradoxes of time and space, and the shifting, unsteady ground that serves as the (non) foundation of each work. Interestingly, some of these complex images and ideas that emphasize multiplicity and instability arise in narratives that at least at first appear straightforward and linear. As noted above, Blanchot believes that Borges's literary approach to the world—the book is the world and the world is a book—might provide the initial comfort that one can theoretically organize and manage the world much as one can do with a book. Yet, the equation of the book and the world creates a mirror relation, a fundamental duplicity, that disrupts any sense of foundation or stability. Blanchot writes, "The world and the book eternally and infinitely send back their reflected images. This indefinite power of mirroring, this sparkling and limitless multiplication—which is the labyrinth of light and nothing else besides—will then be all that we will find, dizzily, at the bottom of our desire to understand" (*BC* 95). In the end, the world escapes and disappears, just like the book. The "labyrinth of light" reveals nothing, as well as the refusal of nothing to appear. In the end, fictions and artifices remain, and those complicated deceptions "make us experience the approach of a strange power, neutral and impersonal" (96). In his essay about Borges, Paul De Man refers to that strange power as a "chaotic reality," which "style is powerless to conquer."[50] With each mirror image and alternate universe in Borges's imaginary worlds, our path becomes less and less sure; yet, in wandering further from the possibility of a destination, we paradoxically come closer to that which escapes our navigation. Turning to "The Garden of Forking Paths," we will see that it provides an especially rich reflection upon the disappearance of the work and the world beyond the structures of the text and the labor of understanding.

"The Garden of Forking Paths" begins with what appears to be an extra-diegetic note—an introduction in the voice of an editor (or similar figure) to the dictation we will soon read. The note refers to an actual historical text, *The History of the World War*, and to an actual historical event: the delay of "an Allied offensive against the Serre-Montauban line" (119). The story grounds us in history before taking us in another direction, suggesting that the official account represents just one narrative possibility for the event, and therefore undermining the grounding of history immediately after providing it. The editorial or critical voice of the note arises in many of Borges's fictions, as he plays with the presentation of his stories as reviews, commentaries, and/or histories, further blurring common distinctions between official history and story, fact and fiction, author and narrator. Regardless, the story begins with a note that tells us that the story has already been told; we already have an explanation for the delay of the attack—"torrential rains"—cited in *The History of the World War* (119). In this way, Yu Tsun's dictation arises, in a sense, after the fact: not only have the war and the specific delay in question passed, but a narrative linking all the details has provided a reasonable explanation for the delay. Yu Tsun's narrative begins at a point where it is not necessary, where it exceeds its narrative purpose. From this perspective, the presentation of Yu Tsun's dictation as a sort of remainder recalls Blanchot's interest in that which begins after all has been accomplished or completed. Like Kafka's "The Burrow," one could say that Borges's story begins at the end, folding back upon and putting into question that end as it excessively moves forward. Yu Tsun's dictation offers an alternate narrative path that both provides an explanation for the delayed attack and remains outside of the demand for an explanation.

Yu Tsun's dictation begins with an ellipsis, indicating that "the first two pages of the statement are missing" (119). The matter of the two missing pages confronts the reader with the arbitrariness of his or her entrance into the text, as we seem to interrupt the dictation by our late arrival. We could apparently enter just about anywhere, and one could imagine that each entrance would provide a different path through the narrative labyrinth. The ellipsis also marks a forceful entry, a rupture, in that it makes us aware that something must have been cut in order for us to begin. The text we read represents a fragment of the entire dictation, although it would be misleading to suggest that the complete document would provide closure and totality, since we have already confronted the possibility of alternate paths to seemingly finished narratives. In other words, the dictation is literally a fragment, but that fragmentation also figuratively points to the impossibility of the whole.[51] As the dictation actually begins, mid-sentence, we are thrown into the developing story of Yu Tsun's work as a spy in the German military. We enter the story at the point when Yu Tsun is discovered by Richard Madden, realizing that the discovery signifies the end of his activity as a spy and the end of his life. Again, we can note the sense that we are beginning at a sort of conclusion, although this particular conclusion will eventually provide a new narrative path that explains the delay in the attack on the artillery park.

Yu Tsun emerges as a Theseus-like character both in terms of his linear narrative style and his focused effort to accomplish a task—a task he must carry out by murdering a man inside a labyrinth. Yu Tsun seeks to master language and space, creating a singular path that connects two end points; his activity demonstrates Blanchot's notion of "a sort of thinning, slimming of space" (*BC* 95). Almost from the beginning of his narrative, we know that Yu Tsun possesses secret information that must be transmitted over an almost insurmountable expanse of space. Although Yu Tsun flees the pursuit of Richard Madden, a captain of the British military who seeks his capture, he has already conceded the final outcome of the chase to his pursuer; so before being arrested or killed, Yu Tsun only desires to communicate the Secret—the location of an artillery park where the British military plans to launch an attack against German forces. Yu Tsun explains, "If only my throat, before a bullet crushed it, could cry out that name so that it could be heard in Germany . . . But my human voice was so terribly inadequate" (120). Quite simply, too much space separates the sender and receiver of the linguistic message; Yu Tsun recognizes the inadequacy of his voice in communicating the integral piece of information to the Leader of the German military. He has a limited amount of time to triumph over the communication gap, putting language's possibilities to *use*—a task he soon accomplishes. On the one hand, Borges points to the alienating character of language by emphasizing the space between two participants in an exchange. But on the other, he seems to offer the possibility of closing the gap, and even mastering language in a sense.

Yu Tsun comes to realize that the space separating himself from the Leader may be traversed if he puts to use the metonymic possibilities of language, creating a sort of linguistic thread connecting the two sides of the exchange. He states, "I vaguely reflected that a pistol shot can be heard at a considerable distance. In ten minutes my plan was ripe. The telephone book gave me the name of the only person able to communicate the information: he lived in a suburb of Fenton, less than a half an hour away by train" (120). The shot of the pistol will become Yu Tsun's voice, even though it is not the shot that will actually be *heard*; rather, the story, or newspaper coverage, of the shot will reach the Leader. In this way, there is a constant folding back onto narrative, or language, despite its apparent inadequacies for the purposes of communication. Furthermore, Yu Tsun plunges into the phone book, with its dizzying amount of slightly varied combinations of letters that form names upon names, in order to overcome the alienating, bifurcating space between sender and receiver. The phone book, by way of the linguistic possibilities it offers, provides Yu Tsun with the necessary tools both to overcome and to employ space in order to transmit his message. While Yu Tsun may not be capable of traversing the literal, geographical gap that separates him from his desired receiver in Germany, he knows he can create a linguistic chain that will travel the distance of an otherwise insurmountable, labyrinthine space. Yu Tsun thus finds a solution to the problem of language (its insufficiency as a means of communication) in language itself.

At the end of his dictation, Yu Tsun tells us of the news-papers that "posed to all of England the enigma of the murder of the eminent Sinologist Stephen Albert by a stranger, Yu Tsun" (127-128). While we might say that newspapers commonly serve to inform the public about current events, we see that this particular newspaper has a dual function, or double meaning. For most, it is simply news, but for the Leader, who "solved the riddle," the paper serves as a secret communication (128). Likewise, the name "Albert" in the article refers to a renowned scholar living in Fenton, England, but it also indicates a city in France where British artillery is hidden. Yu Tsun takes advantage of language's ability to signify two things at once—a fairly clever tactic by a man who, not insignificantly, once worked as an English professor—but the implications of such a strategy ultimately haunt him for the rest of the story. Yu Tsun's step-by-step recitation, his straightforward detective-style narrative, his clever plotting to use language as a tool, his focus on linearity and singularity, and his desire to believe that his life has a single path that he is destined to fulfill—all of these factors certainly work in opposition to a dangerous, plural, uncontainable, shifting language and narrative structure. So if we initially see linguistic and narrative mastery in Yu Tsun's use of the newspaper and the telephone book, we can also predict his defeat, since the very characteristics of language that allow for him to accomplish his task will also prevent him from maintaining mastery over the shifting processes of signification. Ultimately, the forking paths of the labyrinth that Yu Tsun attempts to master will slip beyond his grasp, demonstrating the lingering (yet disappearing) presence of that which exceeds mastery.

Richard Madden plays an integral role in both the initiation and perpetuation of Yu Tsun's story. Because of Madden's desire for "the discovery, capture, perhaps death, of two agents of the German Empire," Yu Tsun's narrative reflects the structure of the chase (119). Yu Tsun must stay one step ahead of his pursuer in order to complete his task, and Madden must *read* and interpret the clues left by the German spy, following the trail left behind. Once Yu Tsun has determined his plan to communicate the message to the Leader, he convinces himself that there exists a single path from the silence of his room in Staffordshire to the noise made by the murder of Stephen Albert. He offers some advice for anyone forced to commit such an act: "*He who is to perform a horrendous act should imagine to himself that it is already done, should impose upon himself a future as irrevocable as the past*" (121, emphasis in original). In order to follow through with Stephen's murder, Yu Tsun convinces himself that there is only one possible "narrative" for his future, a singular path that leads from beginning to end.[52] By committing himself to an irrevocable future, Yu Tsun has determined his narrative before it takes place, and thus rules out the possibility of a different narrative path. In this way, Yu Tsun follows the thread of his supposedly determined future at the same time that Madden must uncover this thread in order to retrace the path forged by Yu Tsun. While the progression of the narrative seems highly deterministic in its apparent absence of choice or divergence from the path, Yu Tsun's language indicates that he is suppressing the labyrinthine structure of his surroundings in order to create linearity. Along with newspapers and telephone books, Yu Tsun mentions airplanes weaving through the sky, blood flowing through his veins, and the deserted street where he "felt [he] was visible and vulnerable—infinitely vulnerable" (121). Yu Tsun appears to recognize the labyrinthine nature of the world, and perhaps life, at the same time that he seeks to limit the space of his narrative in every way—in order that no sense of narrative possibility would suggest an alternate, forking path for his future. One might also note that Yu Tsun passes exclusively through closed spaces—his hotel room, a taxicab, and a train car—before he reaches Stephen's house; perhaps he wants to avoid vulnerability in the branching streets. Throughout the text, Yu Tsun continually attempts to overcome the problem of too much space—whether this refers to the literal space that separates him from the desired recipient of his message, or to a theoretical narrative space that would point to the possibility of different narrative paths for his life. But, as I noted in the case of the telephone book and the newspaper, Yu Tsun's ability to control that which resists containment can only succeed to a certain degree. The presentation of his dictation as a sort of alternate path in itself (an alternate explanation of history) suggests from the beginning of the text that we should be wary of any claims to singularity.

If Yu Tsun works to create a singular path to arrive at an end goal and accomplish his task, suppressing any other possibilities that might exist, Richard Madden must follow suit, tracing and re-enacting Yu Tsun's steps in order to find him. Yu Tsun refers to his exchange with Madden as a "duel," capturing the sense of both play and battle in this strategic clash of two men (121). In the end, Yu Tsun expects Madden correctly to follow the thread he has left behind, tracing each move and closing the gap. And Madden does indeed succeed in reading the clues, as he eventually makes his way through the labyrinth of Yu Tsun's possible actions (which we imagine are multiple from the point of view of Madden) and captures Yu Tsun in Stephen's home. Yet even when "Madden burst[s] in the room and arrest[s]" Yu Tsun, we can assume that he does not understand the meaning of Yu Tsun's crime (127). After all, the newspaper still prints the story, and no one, apparently up until the point of Yu Tsun's dictation, understands the double meaning of the name "Albert." Even Yu Tsun tells us near the beginning of his narrative, "For one instant, I feared that Richard Madden had somehow seen through my desperate plan, but I soon realized that that was impossible" (122). Although Madden appears successfully to read through Yu Tsun's every move, we realize that he has completely missed the "real" meaning behind Yu Tsun's actions. The reader has gone astray, even when he seems on track. Madden navigates the situation masterfully, and finds himself at the center of Stephen's labyrinth-like grounds in position to capture the spy he pursues, yet something clearly eludes his efforts.

The theme of the duel introduced by the adversarial relationship between Yu Tsun and Madden repeats itself in different ways throughout Borges's story. As John T. Irwin notes in *The Mystery to a Solution*, "The cyclically recurring duel between two opposing positions is, of course, an ongoing theme in Borges's work [. . .] the cyclically recurring duel is a function of the reversal mechanism inherent in mutually constitutive oppositions, that it is simply the continuing oscillation between active and passive differential poles as the inferior side seeks to even the score."[53] Irwin comments that the back-and-forth interaction between Madden and Yu Tsun takes place on several levels; not only does it apply to the progression of the chase itself, but it also involves the confusing shifting of winner and loser throughout the story. Madden captures Yu Tsun and wins the chase, yet Yu Tsun succeeds in relaying the message to the German military before his capture. The Germans bomb the artillery park, but we know from the note preceding Yu Tsun's dictation that this attack merely causes a short delay in the British offensive. In other words, the two opposing sides of the duel continually exchange places in terms of empowerment and disempowerment. I would also add to Irwin's reading that there are often strange connections between the two sides of the various oppositions throughout the text. For example, Madden and Yu Tsun both emerge as culturally marginalized figures, fighting for a government that has historically oppressed them. In addition, Yu Tsun and Stephen share a special connection through Yu Tsun's ancestor, Ts'ui Pen. Characters who first appear in an antagonistic relationship bear similarities and become mirror images in some sense; this, along with the "flipping" of the poles of winner and loser, suggests that Borges seeks to undermine the stability and exclusivity of the oppositions. In reflecting one another and switching places, the characters, in their relation, suggest an infinite mirroring that certainly begins to chip away at the boundaries defining their situation and roles.[54] This exemplifies the way that the text escapes and disappears outside of the structures that initially seem to stabilize and define it.

Before considering Ts'ui Pen's novel, *The Garden of Forking Paths*, I would like briefly to return to the character of Stephen in order to provide the context for the discussion of Ts'ui Pen.[55] Stephen Albert first emerges as a more or less arbitrary, but essential, piece of Yu Tsun's message—arbitrary in the sense that he, as a person, has nothing to do with the "meaning" of the message. Because Stephen bears the same name as the location of the secret artillery park, his murder can point to the place Yu Tsun wants to communicate to the German military. But strangely enough, even though Yu Tsun chooses Stephen simply by virtue of his name, the targeted man soon begins to seem less and less arbitrary in relation to Yu Tsun. As Yu Tsun reaches Stephen's house, he explains, "Suddenly, I realized two things—the first trivial, the second almost incredible: the music I had heard was coming from that gazebo, or pavilion, and the music was Chinese. That was why unconsciously I had fully given myself over to it" (123). The skeptical reader may question the triviality of the first "thing" Yu Tsun realizes, since very little remains "trivial" in this story; the significance of the pavilion from which Stephen emerges is later confirmed by the fact that Ts'ui Pen wrote his novel in "The Pavilion of Limpid Solitude" (124). By denying the significance of elements that later reveal themselves as meaningful, Borges brings our attention to the way that every piece seems to fit together in this story—nothing is random, and everything participates in the intricately woven structure of the narrative. Obviously, the Chinese music coming from a home in suburban England, along with the surprising fact that Stephen's greeting is in Yu Tsun's own language, further emphasize the astonishing connection between the two characters. Yu Tsun recognizes the remarkable nature of such occurrences—the man Yu Tsun has "randomly" come to assassinate, Stephen Albert, happens to be a renowned British Sinologist who not only studies Chinese language and culture, but, more specifically, has special expertise in the life and work of Yu Tsun's ancestor, Ts'ui Pen. While Yu Tsun does not further reflect upon this extremely unlikely connection with Stephen Albert, we might note the over-determined, and even contrived, character of the coincidences in the narrative. We can see that Borges has provided Yu Tsun with a narrative path that is anything but arbitrary; in Yu Tsun's narrative, everything makes sense and fits together as perfect pieces of a complete and clearly defined puzzle. By overemphasizing the coincidences of Yu Tsun's story, Borges brings our attention to the ordering function of narrative—or, in other words, to the way that narrative often provides beginnings, ends, connective elements, and a linear, ordered representation of time and space. We begin to see that this is the perfect path for a good story; everything seems to connect in an interesting and meaningful way.

The two men enter a library on Stephen's labyrinth-like grounds, and Stephen begins the conversation by celebrating the life and work of Ts'ui Pen. Yu Tsun immediately offers his thoughts on the novel: "The book is a contradictory jumble of irresolute drafts. I once examined it myself; in the third chapter the hero dies, yet in the fourth he is alive again" (124). Yu Tsun reflects the common opinion of Ts'ui Pen's novel, as the manuscripts recovered from the writer's home had long been considered incomprehensible and unfinished; any reader who approaches the text becomes lost in its confusing weavings. And as for the labyrinth Ts'ui Pen also set out to create, it was never found. But Stephen corrects Yu Tsun, explaining that he has come to the conclusion that the novel *is* the labyrinth:

> In all fictions, each time a man meets diverse alternatives, he chooses one and eliminates the others; in the work of the virtually impossible-to-disentangle Ts'ui Pen, the character chooses—simultaneously—all of them. He *creates*, thereby, "several futures," several *times*, which themselves proliferate and fork. That is the explanation for the novel's contradictions. (125)

In Ts'ui Pen's novel, *The Garden of Forking Paths*, rather than creating a single narrative that determines the movement and the space of the novel, he proposes multiple, seemingly contradictory narratives that disrupt any sense of linearity, chronology, singularity, or coherence. To clarify, none of the narratives is given priority in the greater scheme of the novel; rather, the different paths represent parallel *times* that perhaps converge or diverge throughout the space of the text. In this way, the narrative branches out in various directions, and a given character may simultaneously explore each direction, thus enacting several distinct narrative paths at once.

The novel resembles a physical labyrinth, in that a person traveling through a labyrinth faces many alternatives in terms of the path he or she chooses to take; in an especially well-constructed and complicated labyrinth, we imagine that a person might continually retrace his or her steps, reach the same point from different orientations, and get lost in the seemingly infinite possibilities for movement in such a space. Clearly, a labyrinth of this kind could not be solved simply by turning left at every opportunity to do so. And with this in mind, we see why no one (barring Stephen) understands Ts'ui Pen's book; his novel refuses to let the reader solve its enigma by going left at every turn, following a single path.

This labyrinthine space promotes wandering rather than the arrival at a singular destination. But for this reason, the reader's attempts at comprehension are stifled by the seeming absence of order; like Theseus, the reader relies on mastery when finding his or her way through a text, and getting lost seems to constitute failure. Stephen, of course, eventually uncovers the order of Ts'ui Pen's labyrinth-novel, but there remains an important difference between him and Theseus. Rather than navigating a single path through the labyrinth that would allow him to reach a destination, Stephen's reading of *The Garden of Forking Paths* establishes the order found in its multiplicity. Stephen does not seek to reduce the novel, forging a single path while letting the others bifurcate into the distance; rather, his reading, or imposition of order, attempts to maintain the branching structure. The question becomes whether or not he can impose understanding and structure without destroying the endlessly wandering nature of the text.

Blanchot tells us, referring to the Biblical story of Lazarus, that the reader calls the work forward, allowing it to *be*:

> Reading does not produce anything, does not add anything. It lets be what is. It is freedom: not the freedom that produces being or grasps it, but the freedom that welcomes, consents, says yes, can say only yes, and, in the space opened by this yes, lets the work's overwhelming decisiveness affirm itself, lets be its affirmation that it is—and nothing more. (*SL* 194)

In this way, the reader plays a profound role in the *coming about*, or *becoming*, of the work. Just as Stephen's reading of Ts'ui Pen's novel allows, perhaps for the first time, the infinite weavings of the work to *be*, the reader frees the work from a writer and from the impossibility of writing. Yet, at the same time, "what answers the call of literary reading is not a door falling open or becoming transparent or even getting a bit thinner. It is, rather, a ruder stone, better sealed, a crushing weight, an immense avalanche that causes earth and sky to shudder" (*SL* 195). Blanchot warns us not to assign too much power to reading—as if it were able to uncover the hidden work within the material book. Rather, when the reader approaches the work in order to let it be, he or she feels forcefully excluded, perceiving the infinite disappearance of the work beyond his or her grasp. The reader does not have access, but, instead, opens a space where one perceives that to which we can never have access. But Blanchot insists that reading is still a moment of power, in that the reader calls the work forward and allows for the affirmation of the work in its very disappearance. Returning to Ts'ui Pen's *The Garden of Forking Paths*, we see that Stephen partakes in the form, measure, and power of reading by uncovering the fundamental order of the text; he makes the text appear in the light of day. But paradoxically, it is only Stephen's revelation concerning the labyrinthine structure of the text which ultimately allows the work to recede away from comprehensibility, containment, and measure. Stephen indeed imposes order, but an understanding of that order remains essential when considering the way that the novel evokes an invisible labyrinth and disappears beyond any effort to master it.

Stephen explains that Ts'ui Pen's novelistic labyrinth works as an image of time rather than space, in the sense that the multiplicity of times provides a means for transgressing spatial limitations—whether we think in terms of the space of the book itself, or the space of an enclosed labyrinth. Ts'ui Pen's temporal conception of the labyrinth seeks to eliminate the walls and constraints of the artifice. Stephen shows how the novel functions with an example: "Fang, let us say, has a secret; a stranger knocks at his door; Fang decides to kill him. Naturally, there are various possible outcomes—Fang can kill the intruder, the intruder can kill Fang, they can both live, they can both be killed, and so on. In Ts'ui Pen's novel, *all* outcomes in fact occur; each is the starting point for further bifurcations" (125). With this notion of a branching in time where all possibilities are realized, the novel can theoretically bifurcate infinitely, rather than functioning within the limits of a linear narrative path that begins on the first page and ends on the last. Stephen explains that when he first tried to conceive of an infinite book, he could only come up with a sort of circularity:

> The only way I could surmise was that it be a cyclical, or circular, volume, a volume whose last page would be identical to the first, so that one might go on indefinitely. I also recalled that night at the center of the *1001 Nights*, when Queen Scheherezade (through some magical distractedness on the part of the copyist) begins to retell, verbatim, the story of the 1001 Nights, with the risk of returning once again to the night on which she is telling it—and so on, *ad infinitum*. (125)[56]

Stephen is on the right track here, in the sense that he approaches the question of the infinite text through a temporal model, rather than a spatial one. As Irwin explains in *The Mystery to a Solution*, Borges is critical of the spatial *mise en abyme* that functions as an infinite reflection because it proposes a *regressus in infinitum*—"the continuing diminution in the size of these representations (nested one within another) brings us to a vanishing point where representation becomes meaningless."[57] Contrary to this, the temporal model of self-inclusion, as exemplified by Stephen's example of the *1001 Nights*, does not *minimize* the contained representation, but rather, enacts a rereading that is both the same and different from the prior reading. Irwin confirms:

> The difference between the work and its temporally included self-representation is not a difference of physical size or detail, as in the case of spatial self-inclusion, since obviously there are just as many words in the second reading of the text as in the first. Rather it is a difference of two (or more) separate times of reading that cannot be made to coincide no matter how exactly the text is repeated.[58]

While Ts'ui Pen's novel in some ways resembles the temporal self-inclusion of the proposed story of the 1001 Nights in the middle of the *1001 Nights*, his concept of infinite bifurcation resists the notion of self-inclusion. Rather than turning back in on itself, achieving a sort of temporal infinity through repetition, Ts'ui Pen's novel points to the "outside." Ts'ui Pen creates a small-scale model, or synecdoche, for the layering of multiple, coinciding times in order to point the reader in a certain conceptual direction. He must know that his novel cannot conceivably represent all possible outcomes for his characters, but through its temporal model of infinitely bifurcating narrative paths, it can *point* to the possibilities not contained in the space of his book. In some sense, this might not seem especially innovative when considering that most novels suggest time which precedes and follows the actual events represented in the narrative. But, we must consider the way that narrative does indeed present limitations to the reader, as it determines what is known and what exists within the world of the text. In an attempt to subvert these limitations, Ts'ui Pen creates a structure where the novel becomes only a representative piece of a greater fabric of narratives which remain unwritten. Since his novel proposes *all* narrative possibilities, even if it cannot represent all of them, the world of the text, in a sense, exceeds the world represented by the text. So Ts'ui Pen's novel overtly recognizes its own limitations—the inability fully to represent the temporal labyrinth—but it seeks to overcome these limitations by pushing narrative beyond its own possibilities.

The Garden of Forking Paths evokes Borges's Aleph, in the sense that Ts'ui Pen encourages the reader to see the endless in the singular, or the infinite fabric of time and space in the finite and confusing collection of manuscripts. Turning briefly to "The Aleph," the narrator Borges descends into the cellar of an acquaintance to perceive "one of the points in space that contain all points."[59] As he sits in the enclosed, dark space of the cellar, wondering if he has been tricked into entrapping himself in this underground prison, Borges sees the infinite Aleph. "In that unbounded moment, I saw millions of delightful and horrible acts; none amazed me so much as the fact that all occupied this same point, without superposition and without transparency. What my eyes saw was *simultaneous*; what I shall write is *successive*, because language is successive" (283). When applying the concepts of a chronological, singular time and a measurable, defined space, the image of the Aleph simply does not make sense. In this example, it seems that the tendency to figure infinity as an endlessly extending time or space still fails to transcend the limiting concepts of time and space. In other words, time that never starts or stops, and space that contains no outer limits, remain temporal and spatial notions of that which has no time or space. With the image of the Aleph, Borges reverses this mode of thinking by offering a single moment of time that paradoxically contains *all* time, and likewise, a single point in space that possesses *all* space. In this way, our common perceptions of time and space do not apply; time no longer accumulates in seconds and minutes, and space no longer expands across meters or miles. In this specific reflection upon infinity, Borges encourages us to see the endless in the singular, to perceive *all* as a part of one. In the words of Blanchot, the Aleph represents "the world corrupted into the infinite sum of its possibilities" (*BC* 95). While Ts'ui Pen's novel cannot match the mystical existence of the Aleph, his project offers a sort of Aleph by representing an infinite layering of space and time within the very finite realities of his manuscript and his life. Yes, it points "out" beyond the narrative paths actually represented in the text, but it simultaneously relies upon the perception of the endless in the singular, the infinite within the seemingly definite boundaries of a limited space and time. As Borges's narrator in the Aleph notes, the representation of such a concept remains impossible, given the temporal and spatial character of language. Ts'ui Pen's labyrinth takes shape as writing on paper, and Stephen's reading of a section of the text to Yu Tsun confirms the fact that reading necessarily provides a chronological order to the conceptually simultaneous sections of the text. But it is precisely the inability to be faithful to the endless and timeless character of the work—for both writer and reader—that affirms the disappearance of *The Garden of Forking Paths* beyond the labor that makes it appear.

Ts'ui Pen's project plays with the limits of possibility, coming up against those limits perhaps as a means of touching upon that which escapes possibility. When John Barth writes about Borges's reference to the 602nd night of *1001 Nights*, he describes it as "an image of the exhaustion, or attempted exhaustion, of possibilities—in this case literary possibilities."[60] *The Garden of Forking Paths* is also an image of exhaustion (even if Stephen denies the novel's resemblance to the 602nd night). Ts'ui Pen attempts to write a novel that exhausts narrative possibilities by writing a text where "*all the outcomes occur*" and "each is the starting point for further bifurcations" ("GF" 125). Following Barth's notion of exhaustion, Ts'ui Pen's novel implicitly asks us to imagine a literary universe where all of the stories have been told. That same universe takes shape in Borges's Library of Babel, which contains "all possible combinations of the twenty-two orthographic symbols (a number which, though unimaginably vast, is not infinite)—that is, all that is able to be expressed in every language."[61] In Hegelian terms, we have arrived at the end of literature, but Borges, Barth, and Blanchot all seem to suggest that literature perhaps begins again with its end, precisely in its inability to begin anything anew. While Ts'ui Pen's novel proposes a model that exhausts narrative possibilities, that model also suggests the impossibility of arriving at that point of exhaustion. In effect, Stephen's proposition that "*all the outcomes occur*" implies the possibility of a whole, but, since "each [outcome] is the starting point for further bifurcations," the whole always lies at an infinite distance. At one point, Stephen specifically refers to Ts'ui Pen's work as an "inexhaustible novel" (127). Ts'ui Pen's narrative model is masterful; he manages to create a novel that in some sense exceeds the limits of its own construction. But his mastery necessarily takes both writer and reader to a point where the very essence of the work turns away and disappears, leaving them perpetually wandering towards an impossibly distant destination. For that reason, writer and reader are always simultaneously completing and renewing their journey, experiencing exhaustion in the endlessness of the end.

Clearly, Ts'ui Pen's novel has metaliterary implications and speaks, more specifically, to Yu Tsun's narrative. In typical Borgesian fashion, as Blanchot puts it, "the book is in principle the world [. . .], and the world is a book" (*BC* 95). We see the mirroring of the book and the world take place at the level of Yu Tsun's narrative, as the concept guiding Ts'ui Pen's novel seeps into Yu Tsun's experience with Stephen. Barrenechea remarks in *Borges the Labyrinth Maker* that in "The Garden of Forking Paths," "the fiction overflows its enclosure and contaminates the supposed reality which becomes as chaotic and strange."[62] The mirroring of book and world becomes most apparent as Stephen begins to explain the way that the novel serves as a riddle for Ts'ui Pen's conception of time in the universe:

> *The Garden of Forking Paths* is an incomplete, but not false, image of the universe as conceived by Ts'ui Pen. Unlike Newton and Schopenhauer, your ancestor did not believe in a uniform and absolute time; he believed in an infinite series of times, a growing, dizzying web of divergent, convergent, and parallel times. That fabric of times that approach one another, fork, are snipped off, or are simply unknown for centuries, contains *all* possibilities. In most of those times, we do not exist; in some, you exist but I do not; in others, I do and you do not; in other still, we both do. In this one, which the favouring hand of chance has dealt me, you have come to my home; in another, when you come through my garden you find me dead; in another, I say these same words but am an error, a ghost. (127)

Near the end of the passage, Stephen applies Ts'ui Pen's theory to his own life and to that of Yu Tsun, seemingly as a means to exemplify the way the theory would actually play out in a concrete situation. Stephen expresses gratitude for the specific time he is currently experiencing with Yu Tsun, while acknowledging that it represents only one of many possibilities in the universe proposed by Ts'ui Pen. As readers, we certainly have the sense, though, that Stephen's example goes beyond the realm of the hypothetical. This becomes more apparent with Yu Tsun's response to Stephen, which lends itself to at least two plausible readings. Yu Tsun asserts, "In all [. . .] I am grateful for, and I venerate, your re-creation of the garden of Ts'ui Pen" (127). First, one could imagine that Yu Tsun needs to continue to cover up his murderous intentions and therefore feigns a misunderstanding of Ts'ui Pen's theory in order to maintain the sense that he poses no threat to Stephen. Clearly, as Stephen points out, nothing would be true in all futures. But it is also important to note that Yu Tsun has struggled with the implications of narrative choice throughout the story and desperately tries to convince himself that a single path determines his future. As he learns more about Ts'ui Pen's book, he has an increasing sense of uneasiness and twice refers to a strange "pullulation" inside his body (126, 127). He eventually perceives that "the dew-drenched garden that surrounded the house was saturated, infinitely, with invisible persons. Those persons were Albert and myself—secret, busily at work, multiform—in other dimensions of time" (127). Yet, as Yu Tsun conveys earlier in the narrative, "*He who is to perform a horrendous act should imagine to himself that it is already done, should impose upon himself as future as irrevocable as the past*" (120, emphasis in the original). With this in mind, we might conclude that Yu Tsun's response to Stephen's explanation of their encounter reflects his hesitation to believe in a world where one's future *and* its opposite exist. Interestingly, as Stephen corrects Yu Tsun's misunderstanding, he also falls into the trap of not considering all of the possibilities. After Yu Tsun suggests that he admires Stephen's work in all futures, Stephen replies, "Not in all [. . .]. Time forks, perpetually, into countless futures. In one of them, I am your enemy" (127). Stephen does not appear to realize that in at least one of these futures, Yu Tsun both appreciates Stephen's work on Ts'ui Pen's garden *and* is the enemy.

By the end of Yu Tsun's dictation, we certainly have the sense that the world of the characters mirrors Ts'ui Pen's labyrinth-novel. From that perspective, Yu Tsun's dictation represents one specific future out of many possible times where he encounters Stephen. In this one, Yu Tsun is an intruder who knocks at Stephen's door in order eventually to kill him. This path parallels the story of Fang that Stephen uses to elucidate the apparent contradictions of Ts'ui Pen's novel and further suggests the mirroring relation of book and world. Fang's story involves a secret, a stranger at the door, and murder, although Stephen explains that the roles and events are interchangeable when considering the multiplicity of times. But the mirroring does not stop at the relation between Ts'ui Pen's novel and Yu Tsun's experience of the world. It also has implications for Yu Tsun's narrative (and thus for the reader), which is, at this point, coming to a very tidy end. Yu Tsun recounts shooting Stephen in the back and then puts all of the pieces together for his reader, explaining why he shot an innocent man and how that man's name served to communicate the secret message to the Leader. We thus reach the end of the mystery and appear to have the necessary information to close the case. But Borges's text clearly undermines that sort of an ending even before we get there—especially since he seems to identify his story with Ts'ui Pen's novel by giving it the same name. The repetition of the story's title within the text creates a sort of mirror that encourages the reader to meditate upon the way that the text and the metatext reflect one another. The relationship of the two eventually points to an infinite circularity: Borges writes a story called "The Garden of Forking Paths" about a novel, *The Garden of Forking Paths*; this novel provides a sort of key for reading "The Garden of Forking Paths" about *The Garden of Forking Paths*, ad infinitum. This recalls Blanchot's description of our experience of the infinite in Borges's work: "This indefinite power of mirroring, this sparkling and limitless multiplication—which is the labyrinth of light and nothing else besides—will then be all that we will find, dizzily, at the bottom of our desire to understand" (*BC* 95).

As we see Ts'ui Pen's novel in Yu Tsun's narrative, and vice versa, we might imagine being other readers at other times, reading other narratives that fit together less perfectly; and in that knowledge, we can feel the story slipping through our grasp. It seems even more relevant at this point that the story began with an editorial note that identified it as an alternate narrative path through the already written fabric of history. While Yu Tsun's dictation provides an interesting, tidy path through the labyrinth, Borges's story encourages us to acknowledge the endless expanse of possible narratives that disappear as soon as one chooses a particular path. Yu Tsun tells us in the final line of his dictation that even though the Leader received his message, "He does not know (no one can know) my endless contrition, my weariness" (128). Yu Tsun's regret seems to suggest his recognition of choice, of other narrative possibilities, despite his prior insistence to the contrary; other versions of himself theoretically made other, less burdensome choices. And his weariness points to the fact that the end of his task did not provide repose. Although Yu Tsun manages a Theseus-like feat—in both accomplishing and masterfully narrating his mission—he remains restless, fully aware of the countless paths extending in other directions and of the impossibility of making them disappear by choosing a singular, effective path. And in like manner we arrive at the end of Borges's story, unable to feel satisfied and convinced by our readerly mastery, no matter how clear our conclusions seem. We have navigated the labyrinth, perhaps only to experience our inability to do anything but endlessly wander.

Chapter 4: The Disappearing Act of Louis-René des Forêts's Bavard

If nothing else, when confronted with a *bavard*, or non-stop talker, the listener can feel certain that his or her presence remains a necessary and integral part of the tireless movement of language. Clearly, the listener's role is not entirely engaged or active—a simple feigning of attention provides the illusion of interaction and gives the *bavard*'s chatter a target. Blanchot explains that a sort of polite and indifferent listener best fulfills the needs of the *bavard*, since "he who listens excessively reveals the man who only wants to chatter away, that is to say, speak in excess."[63] The listener is ideally as carefree and distracted as the *bavard* when it comes to "meaningful" communication; "good" listeners threaten to reveal the *bavard*'s secret indulgence of his or her vice. Even if the listener recognizes the pointlessness of the *bavard*'s chatter, the pressure to remain polite will likely prevent a bold interruption of the endless talking. Blanchot explains, "one doesn't walk away from a *bavard*; it's even one of the rare experiences of eternity, reserved for the everyday man" (172). In this way, the *bavard* traps the listener with his or her ability barely to take a breath, playing upon the listener's reluctance to interrupt, or abandon, the seemingly infinite stream of language. As superfluous as a *bavard*'s listener might seem, the limitless talk that emanates from the lips of one who generally communicates nothing of real significance relies upon the impression of exchange. The *bavard* needs a willing participant, even if the *bavard* appears to talk with no regard for that person. We often have the feeling that the *bavard* attempts to fill space and silence when layering word upon word; in a way, these desperate and unsuccessful efforts reflect the inherent problems of communication. From this point of view, the listener's presence in the face of empty chatter points to the gap that necessarily separates all speakers and listeners. For the *bavard*, the production of words and phrases in an uninterrupted flow secures and perpetuates his or her most essential act, at the same time that this domination of the conversation suggests the graver impossibility of communicating something "meaningful." And in turn, the listener recognizes the futility of extracting meaning from discourse that exposes its lack of interest in meaning as it rattles on. In this way, the listener's role mirrors that of the *bavard* because it exceeds any communicative value—the listener need not understand, interpret, relate to, or respond to the *bavard*, but rather should simply turn a careless ear in his or her direction. Anything more would prove pointless, since the *bavard*'s chatter promises nothing more than emptiness.

In Louis-René des Forêts's *The Bavard*, the reader participates in such a conversation. We know from *The Space of Literature* that Blanchot sees the role of the reader in a way that parallels the listener of a *bavard*—light and careless, but necessary, as he or she serves to relieve writing (or talking) from the burden of one who experiences his or her disappearance in the movement of language. But the reader's carefree approach often takes a turn when he or she perceives the book as a stone, behind which lies the dead Lazarus. We want to call him forward, to bring death and absence into the light of day. And, interestingly, we likely take this same turn while reading des Forêts's text. Despite the fact that the narrator reveals himself from the beginning of the text as a *bavard*, we fall into the trap of reading with interpretive purpose, as if it were impossible, or just too difficult, to read the chatter *as* chatter—as empty, and lacking in significance. We want it to *mean* something, to appear to us, to make sense. Of course, the narrator manipulates us into such a reading, perhaps as a tactic for holding our attention, as we serve an integral role, simply by virtue of our presence, in his talking. He creates the impression of an "I" who confesses, expresses, and confides, which encourages us to forget the nature of his language. Indeed, by the end of the text, the *bavard* compares himself to a conjuror who exposes his trick:

> [He's] moved merely by a delight in destroying what he has created and blighting the enthusiasm he has aroused, and so he lays all his cards on the table, making his subtlest tricks seem commonplace, relishing the disappointment of those whom he had astounded, coming down of his own free will from the pinnacle on which his dupes had set him, eagerly watching for the first flicker of disillusionment in their eyes.[64]

After "conjuring" something up, making something appear to us as if it were real, the *bavard* reveals the fraudulence of the act, and of himself. Nothing was ever there—only the illusion—and the *bavard* refuses us the satisfaction of ending the narrative with the illusion intact. What has appeared over the span of roughly one hundred pages disappears with the narrator's final confession that he has talked merely for the sake of talking. And the reader is left to ponder whatever it is that remains after everything has disappeared—the narrator, the narrative, and our imagined role as reader. But, before we reach this point, I would like to consider the narrative game itself—the one that ensnares us, pulls us through the text, and tricks us into believing that we have something before us, under our eyes.

It would seem that the narrator tells us everything we need to know from the first pages of the text. We are directly warned not to invest much in his words, since he almost immediately discloses the nature of his pointless talking and the way he wishes to use us, as readers, to fulfill his desire. He describes the general tendencies of a *bavard* and encourages us to reflect upon our role in the face of such tendencies:

> That he should feel the need to speak and yet have nothing to say, and moreover that he cannot satisfy this need without the more or less tacit complicity of a companion chosen by him, if he's been free to choose, for qualities of discretion and endurance, these facts are worth pondering over. This fellow has nothing whatsoever to say, and yet he says a thousand things; he doesn't really mind whether his interlocutor agrees with or dissents from him, and yet he cannot do without him, although he wisely requires from him only a purely formal attention. (12)

Since the narrator identifies himself as a *bavard*, these characteristics necessarily pertain to him; he offers his narrative as *bavardage* and identifies his reader's "purely formal" role. Therefore, from this point in the text, the narrator makes us aware that neither the "I" nor the content of the narrative should be understood as anything more than the result of a tendency to chatter. In addition, the reader could be any reader, as long as he or she keeps reading, in order that the *bavard* can keep "talking." As readers, we are anonymous, and our interpretive efforts are rejected even before they might begin. After all, there's no point in interpreting a narrative that discloses its lack of substance and its singular goal of simply perpetuating itself for as long as possible. And yet the narrator engages us in a direct way, which brings attention to our role in the narrative, and perhaps invites us out of the anonymity we commonly experience as readers of narratives that neglect explicitly to acknowledge our presence. Somehow, in directly dismissing us, the *bavard* has welcomed us into his narrative, and we perhaps begin to forget that we are not supposed to give credence to anything he says.

The *bavard* openly observes the reader's presence throughout his narrative, and even anticipates the questions, challenges, and critiques that the reader may or may not have. In doing so, he presents himself as an extremely self-conscious *bavard* who exposes the inherent problems of such a mode of talking before the reader raises any objections. This technique of continual self-critique both gives the impression of an uncompromising honesty and silences the reader by intervening before he or she can voice a concern. The *bavard* explains, "A coward conceals the truth under the ambiguous shield of insolence or banter: you despise me, reader, but you can surely see that I'm exaggerating my vices: it's up to you to work out a compromise; nothing prevents you from taking all this as the invention of an exhibitionist whose actions, if not his thoughts, are ingenuous and blameless" (11). By giving voice to the reader's presumed objections, the *bavard* accomplishes a variety of feats: he gives the impression of conversational exchange while maintaining his flow of language; he manipulates the reader into feeling that his or her concerns are addressed; he distances the reader by assuming an antagonistic relationship with him or her; he creates the illusion of total self-exposure and thereby convinces the reader that nothing remains concealed. As a self-proclaimed *bavard*, the narrator cunningly displaces the reader's efforts to imagine what he might not be saying, what he might be hiding. As readers, we feel that the narrative is exhaustive—the *bavard* tells *all*. His labyrinthine trains of thought often refuse the pauses commonly afforded by appropriate punctuation, and convince us that he follows any narrative path that might remotely connect with his point. And, like the listener of a *bavard*, we realize that we fulfill a purpose for this non-stop talker—any opportunity to participate in this "conversation" actively has disappeared, or at least remains unnecessary. At the same time, though, the impression that the narrator creates of total self-disclosure begins to lure us into believing in the earnestness of what he communicates. Paradoxically, he identifies himself as a *bavard*, and so encourages us to dismiss the value of what he says, but his confessional-style self-identification creates a sense of openness and honesty. And we begin to entertain the possibility, perhaps unwittingly, that just this one time the *bavardage* might break with one of its most essential characteristics: its meaninglessness.

Des Forêts's *The Bavard* clearly and self-consciously inscribes itself within a tradition of confessional literature, from Jean-

Jacques Rousseau's *Confessions* to Fyodor Dostoevsky's *Notes from Underground* to Michel Leiris's *Manhood*. While Dostoevsky's note at the beginning of his text clarifies that "Both the author of the notes and the *Notes* themselves are, of course, fictional," Rousseau and Leiris seem to invite the reader into the autobiographical nature of the narrative by suggesting the identification of first-person narrator and author.[65] Philippe Lejeune examines both of these latter texts in *Le pacte autobiographique*, where he defines autobiography as a "*Retrospective story in prose that a real person makes of his own existence, putting emphasis on his or her individual life, and in particular, on the history of his personality.*"[66] He goes on to explain that "In order for a text to be an autobiography (and intimate literature in general) there must be an identification of *author*, *narrator*, and *character*" (15, emphasis in original). Lejeune, of course, admits that serious questions and problems arise with such claims to identification that traverse the diegetic levels of the text; but regardless, we read these autobiographical texts with the aim of observing, and even solidifying, the relationship of the author and the protagonist whom he identifies as himself. In the case of Dostoevsky's text, we are warned not to equate author and narrator in a literal way, but any scholar of Dostoevsky would recognize the author in his anti-hero and therefore acknowledge the autobiographical aspects of his confessional text. Dostoevsky also explains in the note that people such as the Underground Man exist in society, which encourages the reader to recognize this narrator among (or "underneath") the people he or she confronts in everyday life.[67]

How does *The Bavard* fit into this tradition? Blanchot argues that "We are not in the presence of one of these characters of

Dostoevsky, inveterate talkers who, from a desire of provocative confidence, offer themselves at every instant in order better to shut up" ("PV" 165). Rather, we ultimately have the impression that the *bavard* feigns confidence and provokes us by revealing what we might want him to reveal—regardless of its truth. While Dostoevsky's Underground Man frustrates the reader with his continual contradictions, I would suggest that in the confession, Dostoevsky does indeed attempt to expose something inherent or profound about his character's nature. After all, Dostoevsky offers his text as a sort of study into the psyche of underground men in general—a frame of mind produced by certain societal and intellectual trends. In contrast, the *bavard* ultimately confesses or reveals *nothing*, as his narrative emerges as a sort of game that playfully drags us along, simply for the enjoyment of the chase, so to speak. With this in mind, Leiris's *Manhood* invites comparison with *The Bavard* because the first-person narrator discusses the relationship of confession, or self-expression, with the refusal of silence. Blanchot mentions the section of Leiris's text where "the writer finds no other reason for his desire to confess than the refusal to say nothing, showing that the most irrepressible speech, that which knows no limit or end, has for its origin its own impossibility" ("PV" 165). This passage in *Manhood*, upon which Blanchot comments, certainly relates to the *bavard*'s mode of communication. As we shall see, des Forêts's text continually plays upon the relationship of speech and silence, suggesting that speech refuses silence at the same time that it reaffirms it—a complicated paradox that reveals the impossibility of truly distinguishing the seemingly opposing poles of the continual production of words and wordlessness. Despite the similarities between *Manhood* and

The Bavard, Blanchot notes that the defining difference between the two modes of first-person narration lies in the status of the "I" in the text. In the case of Leiris's "I," "We maintain the impression of being able to interrogate him and even to hold him accountable; someone is there who responds to what he affirms; there is a promise, and like a sermon of truth, we can take from it, for ourselves, faith and certitude" (167). In contrast, the *bavard*'s negation of the "truth" of his narrative suggests that he has only constituted his identity through a language that promises nothing—a language derived from emptiness, interested only in perpetuating itself. Therefore, the "I" of *The Bavard* slips into the profound fictionality of the text, revealing not his vices and secrets, but his absence. At the same time, this absence, or disappearance, relies upon the magic trick—the illusion of an "I" that takes shape over the span of the narrative.

The *bavard* announces from the beginning of his narrative that he "pride[s] himself on having small liking for confessions," and claims that such an act is in contrast with his nature ("B" 10). His inability to confide in his friends causes them to conclude that he is "silence itself"; furthermore, this silence creates the impression of a compelling secrecy (10). The *bavard* admits that he enjoys the interest of those who believe him to be in possession of an intriguing secret, but then suggests that he will deny the temptation of treating his reader in the same way. "But if I let my zeal run away with me I shall end by ascribing to myself ulterior motives which I have never had, in order to pass for a sincere man who does not seek to spare himself humiliations. It is therefore not for the pleasure of talking about myself that I have taken up my pen, nor yet to show off my literary gifts" (10). The *bavard* speaks against his own tendency to lose himself in the creation of an image—whether this image provides the impression of secrecy or uncompromising self-exposure—and in doing so appears to set himself against the tradition of confessional literature. The feigning of sincerity recalls a common critique of Rousseau's *Confessions*, the pleasure of talking about oneself directly references Dostoevsky's Underground Man, and the exposition of literary gifts suggests Leiris's attempt to combine autobiography with poetry.[68,69] The *bavard* continually and openly battles the tendencies of confession and does not hesitate to critique himself in moments of overwrought sincerity, self-indulgence, or artful rhetoric. The narrator's self-deprecating tone and his insistence on exposing the weaknesses of his confession draw the reader into the conversation—even if we must practice an enduring patience while wading through a sea of irrelevant details and exhausting tangents. The *bavard* creates an aura of conversation by distinguishing himself from his literary predecessors and engaging the reader with an informal banter that doesn't seem to take itself too seriously. The *bavard* is witty, peculiar, self-aware, and engaging; we listen to his monologue with interest and curiosity. And, rather than anonymous readers, we become confidants, ready and willing to put aside what we know of the narrator and his manner of talking, in order to receive his confession in good faith. Almost impossibly, even as we experience the loquaciousness of his narrative, we assume that this *bavardage* is more than *bavardage*. If we eventually distinguish the *bavard*'s narrative from other confessional-style texts, it's not until after we invest in the confession. The *bavard* relies upon the narrative mode of confession to solidify the sense of an "I," since this mode generally operates as the intimate expression of a first-person narrator. And he seems to know something about our tendency as readers to depend upon the promise of meaning, which in some ways makes us complicit in his fraudulence. As readers, we also want to have a sense of individual identity, rather than disappearing into the anonymity of the sort of careless and light reading demanded by empty chatter.

Des Forêts's text presents the difficult challenge of figuring out what to do with the narrative once we discover its fraudulence. After all, the narrator eventually tells us that everything he has expressed simply served the purpose of holding our attention, so it doesn't seem to make sense to then go back and read it for meaning. Thematically, though, the narrative continually reflects upon the *bavard*'s inability both to talk and *not* to talk. Whether genuine or fabricated, "real" or made-up, the metaliterary implications of the *bavard*'s narrative illuminate the questions raised by this self-nullifying text. The character of his story—the isolated man who goes to a seaside bar and suffers an attack of chattering, only to be humiliated—reveals something about a text that seems to begin from a point where talking, or writing, is not possible. And, as we have seen, the narrator's ability to engage us, to create an illusion with his confession, sets the scene for the final disappearing act. In other words, in order to show his own absence and the impossibility of talking, the narrator must talk. And in order to demonstrate our exclusion from the text, as readers, we must be encouraged to resurrect Lazarus so as to confront the ruder stone that lies behind him. As the narrator tells a story about trying to locate his voice and to express himself, ultimately realizing the impossibility of talking (and not talking), we read about the conditions that lead the narrative eventually to fold back upon itself and disappear in a sense—along with the narrator and ourselves—as active, empowered, interpretive readers. And so it is with this in mind that we can turn to the confession itself—not so much with the intention of resurrecting meaning from the explicitly meaningless, but in order to consider the way it perhaps reveals something about the excessiveness and powerlessness of language.

The *bavard* begins his narrative: "I often look at myself in the glass"—plunging the text into questions of identity and self-analysis from the first words (9). He admits that this interest in gazing into the mirror reveals his desire to observe a certain singularity in his expression that distinguishes him from others. Although the *bavard* entertains the thought that he is perceived as unique and different, he ultimately concludes: "how can I disguise from myself the fact that I am utterly undistinguished?" (9). Several times in this opening "reflection" the *bavard* refers back to his facial expression while narrating—he notes when certain thoughts cause him to grimace or smile, as if he were actually looking at himself in the mirror during the writing process. We get the sense that the *bavard* is trying to capture the physical aspects of his own identity while transcribing it onto the written page. The *bavard* observes and construes himself through the careful inspection of his own gaze—not always sure what to make of his intentions or motivations, but interested in the process by which he sees and perceives himself and his surroundings. Through this self-examination and confession we expect that the *bavard* will confront the brutal honesty of the mirror, revealing the imperfections, or almost imperceptible details, that often remain hidden. Yet the *bavard*'s first observation concerns the fact that he looks into the mirror and sees his sameness, or even, anonymity. This is the first indication that the reader will have difficulty attaching the narrative to the "I" who narrates, since this person seems to blend into the background, bearing no trace of singularity. The *bavard*'s gaze into the mirror provides us very little insight into the origin of the narrative voice—the "I"—but, instead, demonstrates that the voice appears to arise from a sort of "no one," or "anyone." The *bavard*'s inability to see himself, or his individuality, in the mirror suggests Blanchot's notion of the writer's inability to establish his or her own voice in writing. When describing the neutral, anonymous voice of writing, Blanchot explains, "The writer belongs to a language which no one speaks, which is addressed to no one, which has no center, and which reveals nothing" (*SL* 26). The *bavard* indicates his relation to such a language since he cannot identify the person in the mirror—the person who speaks, narrates, and says "I." Still, the reader proceeds, likely with the hope that the "I" will take shape over the span of the narrative, throughout the narrator's process of confession and self-examination.

The *bavard* proudly claims that his friends believe him to be in possession of a secret, since he has "small liking for confessions," and therefore refuses to reveal anything intimate about himself (10). His silence and inability to confide in others strengthens the idea that the *bavard* maintains a certain anonymity—it seems that no one truly knows him. The interest of his friends provokes the *bavard* to play along by giving the impression that he is holding back a truly dark and compelling revelation. Of course, the *bavard* turns to the reader with his confession, despite the claim that his secret vice remains "quite impossible to confess" to his friends (10). The *bavard* presents this narrative as a breaking of his characteristic silence, even though we will discover that the apparent motivation for his confession involves explaining a dramatic verbal attack that has already destroyed the secrecy of his silence. Here, an important distinction arises between the enactment of a so-called vice, and the explanation of it. While the *bavard*'s friends—along with a crowd of onlookers—have witnessed the narrator's attack, his confession seeks to promote understanding and even sympathy for an uncontrollable urge. With this in mind, the language of the confession apparently serves not to give pleasure or fulfill desire, but rather to elucidate and reveal what the narrator refers to as a disease. In other words, he wants to be able to explain his irrepressible need to chatter without having us mistake his narrative for the same type of language. In addition, to assure us of the genuine nature of his confession, the *bavard* promises, "today I have resolved, with a certain reluctance, to lay aside any studied refinement of form" (10). And when he feels compelled to develop a "literary" description of an atmosphere, he stops himself, for "it would involve breaking the vow I have made to myself not to resort to dishonest literary expedients which repel me" (13). In this way, the narrator claims to approach his confession with a seriousness and honesty that allows for the most "pure" explanation of his sickness—without any other intention than to openly and uncompromisingly communicate with the reader.

The *bavard* begins by detailing the first time he suffered from the urge to speak without stopping. Preceding the attack, he notices a sense of euphoria that appears to come from the beautiful and silent surroundings of the cliffs and the sea. He explains:

> My serenity gave place to a strange excitement which took the form of a frantic need to make a speech immediately, although I felt no concern as to whether this speech would make sense

and even less as to what its theme should be; I was prey to such violent agitation that I sprang to my feet precipitately. However, I never uttered that speech; my lips remained obstinately closed and I stood there in silence waiting for this oratorical thirst to abate of itself. (14)

The *bavard* victimizes himself through his language, referring to frantic need, violent agitation, and an unquenchable thirst, making sure we note that this attack exceeds any rational attempt to control it. He emphasizes the act itself, rather than any concern for content, which shows the priority of the force and movement of language over its communicative purpose. Yet the *bavard* at this time remains impotent: "I wanted to talk and had absolutely nothing to say" (15). At this point, it seems that the *bavard* doesn't quite know how to speak from a place of nothingness—a skill he will later develop—even though he does point out his lack of concern for the subject matter of his speech. In any case, the narrator experiences discomfort and distress, but these feelings last only a short while, and he thinks no more of the attack—probably because it never materializes.

Although the narrator makes the distinction between self-expression—as a form of intimate communication with a listener—and an attack of chattering, he argues that the anguish of repressing either one is the same. In this way, the *bavard* makes a connection between his inability to confide in his friends and his failure to satisfy the desire to speak. He explains that the problems are different, but the result remains the same:

> In my friends' company, the problem was that of self-expression; on the cliffs, merely that of chattering at random, regardless of logic or coherence. It was one thing to be unable

to communicate and thereby to be deprived of the pleasure of pure and sincere friendship, but quite another to suffer from an apparently organic deficiency whose most obvious result was to repress a vice that might be dangerous and was, in any case, sterile, since I did not feel I could derive from it that vital satisfaction that we seek through confiding in another person. But still the two experiences had at least one thing in common: anguish. (16)

Although the *bavard* tells us earlier in his narrative that he enjoys seducing his friends with his compelling silence, he reveals here that this silence causes him to suffer, since he sees his inability to communicate as a barrier to sincere friendship. The *bavard* does not explicitly develop any explanations as to why self-expression and communication remain an impossibility for him, but his desire to connect with others is unsatisfied due to an unavoidable communication gap. Such a situation produces anguish in the *bavard*, and he relates this feeling to that which he experiences when unable to fulfill his need to chatter. According to the *bavard*, unlike the feeling of anguish that results, the desire he feels while alone on the cliffs does not relate to his inability to connect with his friends; yet we will see that when he finally explodes verbally in the bar, it seems to result from the drive to establish intimacy with another person. With this in mind, both silence and chattering (or the unfulfilled need to chatter), for the *bavard*, point to a certain powerlessness in terms of communicating in a meaningful way.

In *What is There to Say?*, Ann Smock develops the question of the inability to speak at length, and specifically addresses the two sides of this problem in the work of des Forêts. The *bavard*'s problem reflects the dual nature of the powerlessness associated with language: he finds it impossible to speak at the same time that he cannot keep from speaking. Smock explains:

> In short, to speak a language in the world of des Forêts is to be lodged between the painful impossibility and the awful probability of your discovery. It's to hang, in other words, between the heartbreaking impossibility that anyone, including you yourself, will ever know you and the terrible likelihood that someday someone will—indeed quite probably a whole jeering crowd and even you yourself.[70]

The *bavard*'s powerlessness on the one hand reveals itself in his inability to communicate with his friends, to express and share himself. The *bavard* is silent because he cannot speak. On the other hand, the *bavard* simultaneously suffers from the inability to silence himself; he chatters from a place of total powerlessness, where the words surge forth uncontrollably and unrestrainedly. Furthermore, the *bavard* desires to speak, to say what he cannot say, especially since it would mean that he could communicate sincerely with his friends; but this desire manifests itself in a sort of talking that simply reveals the other side of his inability. In this way, words, which seem to be the solution, end up creating more distance and demonstrate that the presence of language does not address the problem of silence. In sum, the *bavard* cannot speak, and he cannot *not* speak. The *bavard* speaks a language that no one speaks, without the ability to speak it. And he experiences the extreme solitude that accompanies the speaking of a language without a speaker, much like Blanchot's writer in *The Space of Literature*. Language opens a space where one disappears, but not without longing to reconnect with the world in some way. Even as the *bavard* describes his condition, though, I would argue that we continue reading under the assumption that the *bavard*, in this instance, transcends the problems he shares with us—that his narrative arises out of the ability to express and confess his experiences (of not being able to express or confess). It is not until the end of the text that we must face the fact that this narrative, too, reveals the powerlessness to speak, to share, to confess—not only in its content, but in its performance.

When the *bavard* and his friends enter a crowded and noisy bar, his first reaction is of relief, since he will not be obliged to talk in such an atmosphere. He explains: "it was pleasant to think that I could in all quietude enjoy the pleasure of watching a bit of life without being required to take part in it; all that I wanted now was to stay in one corner, surrounded by smoke and music and laugher and yet solitary, watching avidly and clearsightedly an animate scene in which I alone, to my great satisfaction, took no active part" (20). The *bavard* quietly distances himself from the crowd, simply looking on as the events of the evening unfold. Returning briefly to *What is There to Say?*, Smock refers to the *bavard* as a spectator and a voyeur who celebrates his indifference and detachment from the scene. She writes, "It is a calm disinclination to have any part in all that hubbub or to acknowledge any stake in it—a serene liberty, a blithe irresponsibility with a beautiful edge of insolence, an understated insubordination."[71] The *bavard* here enjoys his anonymity, his ability to disappear into the background and to hold his tongue. It would seem that anonymity sometimes has its benefits, as the *bavard* can sink into passivity and observation, perhaps even with the momentary impression that he is in control of his speech—at this point, he appears to *choose* silence and "personlessness." Yet, as Smock suggests, the *bavard* eventually assumes his role; he emerges from the background and reveals himself for what he is—a *bavard*.

At the point when the *bavard*'s gaze falls upon a beautiful woman dancing with an awkward red-haired man, he senses that she shares his detached relationship with the room full of people. "I immediately had the comforting feeling that there was someone else in the room who, behind an inexpressive mask, fed secretly on the pleasure of others with an avidity as feverish and deliberate as my own" (23-24). Provoked by intrigue and physical attraction, the *bavard* decides to interrupt the dancing of the woman and her partner in order to hold her in his own arms. The woman manages to dismiss her angered partner, and the narrator becomes immersed in the pleasure of the moment. He explains that the woman "succeeded in delivering me from the anguish to which I am condemned almost continuously by the feeling of irremediable loneliness" (28). The *bavard*'s reference to anguish obviously recalls the feelings brought on by his inability to talk—whether in regards to confiding in his friends or satisfying the urge to chatter. Somehow, this stranger in the bar soothes the narrator's anguish and appears to offer the profound connection that has forever eluded him. When the two dancers go to a table to have a drink, the woman's partner returns in order once again to object to her interaction with the *bavard*. After a short struggle with the red-haired man, the *bavard* disengages himself from the situation and simply observes the tension he has managed to create. "I mistook myself for a spectator when it was quite evident that I was one of the actors, the least interesting of the three by reason of the cowardly and passive attitude in which I persisted" (32). The *bavard* envisions himself as an audience member at the theater, as if his role in the unfolding plot remained distinct and separate from his enjoyment as a spectator. We see the *bavard*'s continual tendency to observe himself as an outsider, and as anonymous; he seems to attribute his actions to someone else, which points to a distance between his thoughts, or perceptions, and his active involvement in the scene. The *bavard*'s engagement in self-analysis in this scene parallels the first line of the narrative as he studies himself in the mirror. He sees himself as Other, and therefore can simultaneously judge and serve as the object of judgment—but not quite recognizing himself in his actions. The *bavard* appears to perform for himself in the bar, fulfilling the roles of both actor and audience. One even has the sense that the other characters in the scene merely function as props—the performance revolves around the *bavard* to the extent that anyone or anything else could be cast aside.

Once he regains the woman's attention, the sense of intimacy returns—despite the fact that the two sit in silence as a result of not speaking the same language. The *bavard* welcomes this silence, since, he explains, "I felt that that an exchange of commonplace words might interrupt our ecstasy" (35). The *bavard* has clearly reengaged himself in the moment, claiming his role in the silent interaction with the woman. He feels a certain intimacy with the woman, and admits, "I already caught myself mentally confiding to her certain things about myself which in normal times I should never have considered revealing to my most intimate friend, far less to a person who was practically unknown to me" (35-36). This silent confidence and closeness helps the *bavard* to ease his anguish, but it also apparently compels him finally to satisfy his urge to speak without restraint. Even though he does not have the power to initiate such speech—it arises out of the inability not to speak—we have the sense that it responds on some level to the intimacy he perceives with the woman. The *bavard* has allowed himself momentarily to believe that the abyss separating him from others, and making intimate communication impossible, has been overcome; yet, the chattering that ensues affirms the interval, demonstrates his inability to speak, and ensures his solitude.

As the *bavard* describes the setting of the bar when his attack begins, he focuses on the impression that he has of an audience waiting for him to take the stage in order to publicly reveal and satisfy his most profound desire. Despite the importance of the crowd, the *bavard*'s chattering attack is directed specifically toward the woman whom, he is convinced, represents the opportunity for him to break the lonely silence of his existence. He explains, "It was impossible to remain silent with those eyes upon one; convinced that one could never confide to anybody else the essential things one had to say, and this if one persisted in keeping silent one would lose one's last chance, one naturally sought to seize an opportunity that would not come again" (42-43). The language of the narration suggests that the *bavard* again attempts to distance himself from the singularity or individuality of his feelings and actions. Rather than employing the first person, he turns to the subject "one" as a means of implying that his actions result from a natural human inclination to break from the constraints of solitude in favor of establishing an intimate connection with another person. These efforts at generalization, rationalization, and justification point to the *bavard*'s need to understand an act that appears to be out of his control. This lack of control becomes evident when the *bavard* realizes he is already talking without knowing it: "I had already begun to speak when I become aware of it" (43). It is as if the *bavard*'s mouth began to speak without asking his permission; he is again relegated to the position of observing his own actions, to the extent that he can only acknowledge the words pouring out of his mouth, powerless to slow the hemorrhage. This time, though, the *bavard* realizes his primary role in the scene.

Once aware of his chattering mouth, the *bavard* still claims to have no consciousness of the confessions he makes. "The vital thing for me was to talk, irrespective of what I was talking about. Obsessed by delight at my release I scarcely noticed the appalling things I was saying and was only aware of them through their reflection on the faces of my audience" (45). The *bavard* emphasizes the act of talking, of releasing the burden of silence and solitude. This suggests that the content of the *bavard*'s confession remains unimportant, since any words would apparently fulfill his purpose. Yet the reaction of the audience indicates otherwise, since, from the *bavard*'s perspective, they judge the meaning of the words he produces. The *bavard* eventually admits that he has some awareness of the content of his monologue when he explains that the "sordidness [of the revelations] I deliberately exaggerated out of bravado" (46). What do we make of this contradiction? The *bavard* assures us—as does our understanding of *bavardage*—that he chatters irrespective of what he actually says, but the response of the onlookers, along with his own observations, points to the transgressive nature of the revelations he makes. What does he reveal? And what do these revelations tell us about his character? Probably nothing of real importance. In order to maintain his place on center stage, the *bavard* must hold attention, making sure his listeners don't turn away. This is his essential task, and we, as readers, are in the midst of affirming the *bavard*'s success in performing that task. At this point in the text, and especially after discovering the fraudulence of the *bavard*'s story, we should see ourselves in the audience members; like them, we get caught up in the content, not realizing that it's above all a snare to keep our attention..................

Until this point in the *bavard*'s verbal exposition, he remains convinced that the woman at whom he directs his speech returns his feelings of connection and intimacy. "I was musing without mental reservations on all the secret affinities between this woman and myself, when I was feeling happy at finding her silent, grave, attentive" (49). Again, his thoughts seem not to focus on whatever it is he is actually saying, but on the "secret affinities," or his sense of mutual feelings presumably left silent and unspoken. The speech gains its force and significance from her attention, and from her complicity in his vice. The *bavard* appears to interpret the woman's silence as encouragement and continues, uninterrupted, until he has achieved a moment of "genuine emotion" (49). This climactic moment is followed by a brief silence—a silence that the woman interrupts with loud, unrestrained, humiliating laughter. Obviously, the *bavard*'s illusions of intimacy are shattered, but more importantly, the inability to meaningfully communicate reaffirms itself. The *bavard* recognizes his chattering for what it is—an empty, meaningless, self-indulgent flow of words that makes evident the interval infinitely separating him from the woman, and from everyone else. His relationship, or lack thereof, with the woman becomes painfully clear, and the seeming breaking of silence and solitude proves itself to be illusory. Interestingly, the *bavard* wants to be able to use language to express himself, to reveal his secrets and establish intimacy with others; he feels anguish over his inability to do so. In some sense, he manages to accomplish this task at the seaside bar—not necessarily through the "meaning" of what he says, but through the act of speaking. The *bavard* reveals himself for what he is, but "what he is" can only further distance himself from others. Momentarily, he believes himself to have power over language, since he perceives it to forge a connection with the woman at the bar; in the end, though, the woman's response affirms the *bavard*'s inability to speak. She responds not with words, but with a parallel gesture—uncontrollable laughter.

After the *bavard* discusses the aftermath of the scene at the bar at some length, we arrive at the section of the narrative where he reveals his ruse. When comparing himself to a conjuror, he explains that at some point, one might "exchange the pleasure of enchanting [the crowd] for that of disenchanting them" (90). Rather than leaving us with the illusion he has created, the *bavard* chooses to expose himself, revealing his confession's fictionality as well as his own. As I discussed earlier, we confront a variety of problems once the narrator tells us that his story simply served as a means of holding our attention, and that he only appeared to be confessing his most intimate secrets and vices. Of course, all stories engage in such games to varying degrees—because stories need readers, and readers need a reason to keep reading—but the *bavard* claims that his story was *only* a game, a lie, a trick. Moreover he employs a mode of narrative that lures us into a relation with the "I" of the text. It is for this reason that we, as readers, feel betrayed at the end of the text. I would argue that our sense of betrayal arises not from the *bavard*'s revelation that the content of the confession is fictional, but rather, from our newfound awareness that there is no "I" with whom we have been silently conversing. Even if we have recognized our role as passive listeners of a *bavard* who simply requires our mildly attentive presence, we identify the "I" with a speaker. The text invites us to do so because it presents itself in the form of a first-person confession. At the end of the text, the creation and revelations of the "I" no longer provide the foundation for our reading process—nothing is there, except for empty words that have kept us turning the pages of the book.

So what happens to the status of the narrative preceding this revelation, and moreover, what happens to the "I" to whom we have been patiently listening? Blanchot warns us not simply to see this as a pointless story that the *bavard* invents only to fulfill his urge (even though the *bavard* pushes us to see it this way). Instead Blanchot explains that the *bavard* deceives us, "because this 'I' is already for him a fable—that he must tell us these stories, trying to capture himself in them, and without doubt, keep our attention with them, maintaining with obscurity a relation to the truth by the very indecision of his own lie" ("PV" 170). Similar to the way that the *bavard* attempts to identify himself in the mirror at the beginning of the narrative, he grasps at the traces of an unidentifiable "I" when creating himself through language. The *bavard* tells us (whether we believe him or not) that he cannot identify himself, or establish himself through language; it would therefore be equally problematic for the *bavard* to offer a confession where he affirms his powers of self-expression. In some sense the lie, in its inability to tell the truth, remains more faithful to the conditions of language about which the *bavard* (and des Forêts) tells us. Blanchot later adds, "But his 'I' is so porous that it can't retain itself; it silences all parts, silence that chatters in order to better hide itself, or to better turn itself towards ridicule" (170).

The *bavard*'s "I" recedes into silence and anonymity, and in this way simply becomes a function of the free-flowing *bavardage* directed at a mildly attentive listener. The chatter therefore points to the silence and solitude of the *bavard*—his inability to constitute himself through the "I" of his narrative. As a result, the narrative does not belong to the *bavard*, and it is precisely the unclaimed, unidentified character of the language that opens the text to its absent foundation. From this point of view, the *bavard*'s solitude parallels that of the writer if we recall Blanchot's analysis of the writer's perpetual exclusion from both the world and the work. The *bavard*'s exclusion from the world becomes quite evident if we take any thematic significance from his story, but also if we simply consider the way he antagonizes and dismisses his reader. Perhaps more importantly, the *bavard*'s nullification of his narrative suggests the writer's exclusion from the work. Blanchot writes in *The Space of Literature*, "No one who has written the work can linger close to it. For the work is the very decision which dismisses him, cuts him off, makes of him a survivor, without work" (24). If the *bavard* denies us a relation to the confession and to the "I" who speaks it, he also denies himself this relation and further emphasizes his anonymity and solitude.

The *bavard*'s dismissal of the content of the narrative further emphasizes his inability to confide through "positive" communication and his struggle to capture, through his own gaze, any sense of self. Rather, he embraces his solitude by alienating himself from his reader and from his confession. Interestingly, the *bavard*'s revelation of his narrative game comes with an abrasive, and even "unsportsmanlike," sense of power over the reader. The game feels less fun than mean-spirited, as the *bavard* antagonistically resorts to name-calling and ridiculing. As we have seen, the *bavard* prefers the comparison with a conjuror to demonstrate the ingenuity of both the illusion and the disillusionment involved in his storytelling. One might also note that he again reverts to the third-person, as if not fully able to claim his narrative trick, even in the exposition of his mastery.

> [H]e's moved merely by a delight in destroying what he has created and blighting the enthusiasm he has aroused, and so he lays all his cards on the table, making his subtlest tricks seem commonplace, relishing the disappointment of those whom he had astounded, coming down of his own free will from the pinnacle on which his dupes had set him, eagerly watching for the first flicker of disillusionment in their eyes. (91)

While the *bavard* presents himself as one who creates and destroys, manipulating readers (his dupes), we might see this as a final effort to take power over his language. Rather than giving in to the inability to speak, the *bavard* plays a game that would seem to make of language an act of "his own free will." And rather than facing the humiliating laughter of a listener or reader, the *bavard* turns the tables in an attempt to cease control of his speech; rather than being ridiculed, he ridicules. But language has accomplished nothing here. While the *bavard* succeeds in luring the reader through the text, believing in the "I" that he creates, he has only managed to demonstrate his own anonymity, his reader's anonymity, and the inability of language to say anything at all. The *bavard* makes everything disappear, taking us to the limit of what he is able to do; but this negation gives rise to nothing, since nothing was ever there in the first place, except for the movement of disappearance, which he does not have the power to make disappear.

And still, even after he has revealed his trick with the pride of a magician, the *bavard* rattles on, filling ten more pages with his characteristically tangential and chattering style. He justifies himself, explains certain motivations and intentions, antagonizes his reader, and implicitly encourages us to keep turning the pages. Has anything really changed? Does the reader put down the book after experiencing disillusionment? Do we not still hope for something, anything at all, that would assign a speaker to this vain speech? In the end, our own identity and individuality as readers of meaning, as interpreters, is at risk; we sense the peril of our own disappearance. The *bavard* recognizes our fears and hopes by producing a few agonizing, unanswerable questions for us: "Am I a man, a shadow, or nothing, absolutely nothing? Have I gained any substance through chattering to you all this while? Do you picture me as possessing other organs besides my tongue? Can I be identified with the owner of the right hand that is setting down these words? How are you going to find out?" (98). The *bavard* maintains the impression of power by posing questions to us and playing upon our fears, but such questions also reveal his awareness of the risk of his own disappearance. While the reader does keep reading, perhaps naively, the *bavard* also keeps talking. After making everything disappear, the *bavard* can't seem to stop the chattering. The *bavard* is still failing to see himself in the mirror and has only his fraudulent narrative to cling to. Since the "I" of the text doesn't exist, the power of deceit, of manipulation, of ultimate disillusionment belongs to no one; it arises from language itself—a language that speaks without a speaker. Blanchot points to this same idea: "One speaks. This means: no one speaks. This means: we live in a world where there is speech without a subject that speaks it, a civilization of speakers without speech, aphasic *bavards*" ("PV" 178). Nothing really changes when the *bavard* reveals his lie because speech continues to speak without a speaker; the status of language lies not in its relationship to truth or falsehood (between which we cannot distinguish), but in its dissociation from a speaker. And, from this point of view, all speakers are *bavards*. Therefore, *bavardage* becomes the condition—the disease—of language, and it renders both speaking and reading impotent to make anything appear out of the nothingness of empty words.

Chapter 5: Anonymity and the Neutral in Nathalie Sarraute's *Tropisms*

The first section of Nathalie Sarraute's *Tropisms* begins, "They seemed to spring up from nowhere, blossoming out in the slightly moist tepidity of the air, they flowed gently along as though they were seeping from the walls, from the boxed trees, the benches, the dirty sidewalks, the public square."[72] The language encourages us to imagine creeping ivy or the uncontrollable spreading of vine-like weeds as "they" wind through and around the structures of the town. The moist atmosphere calls them forth, and they come to inhabit any space that allows for their proliferation. Sarraute does not identify the pronoun "they" in the first sentences of her text, and further challenges the reader's attempts to do so by seeming to reassign the pronoun in the second half of the tropism. As we read "They looked closely at the piles of linen in the White Sale display," the "they" becomes human; "they" look through the same store windows in front of which "they" were sprouting through the sidewalk cracks (13). We also need to consider the possibility that "they" refers to the group of people from the beginning of the tropism, even though it seems to describe plant life at first; perhaps the people emerge from their homes and into the streets of the town in a way that suggests the crawling vines of a plant. In any case, the striking anonymity of the text—which characterizes all of Sarraute's *Tropisms*—makes it very difficult to distinguish between different people and things; we might recognize the difference but struggle to find the definitive outlines, boundaries, and qualities that would allow us to identify the characters and objects in the text. The characters—virtually all referred to as "she," "he," or "they"—blend together, denying the reader the opportunity to situate himself or herself in the text by identifying with a perspective or voice that would provide a sense of place and vision.[73] Sarraute's *Tropisms* evokes Blanchot's discussion of the neutral—a space, a mode, a voice founded upon no one, nowhere. In the anonymous space of the nearly indistinguishable fragments that constitute *Tropisms*, the absence of narrative conventions like plot and character shifts focus to the movement of disappearance—the continual slipping away of the text from our grasp.

As discussed in the first chapter of this study, Blanchot refers to "the third person substituting for the 'I'" in *The Space of Literature* in order to discuss the way that the writer's ability to say "I" disappears when writing; the narrative voice emerges, although that voice does not become an empowered substitute, speaking where the writer cannot (28). Blanchot explains, "It does not denote objective disinterestedness, creative detachment. It does not glorify consciousness in someone other than myself or the evolution of a human vitality which, in the imaginary space of the work of art, would retain the freedom to say 'I'" (28). In other words, the substitution marks the disappearance of the speaking subject, an individual consciousness through which the reader perceives the world of the text (regardless of whether the narrative takes the form of a third- or a first-person perspective). In *The Infinite Conversation*, Blanchot expands upon those reflections on the narrative voice and uses Franz Kafka's work to exemplify the way that distance and strangeness may speak in a text, rather than a subject. He presents the narrative voice in Kafka's work in direct contrast to a narrative perspective based on the ability to examine and present the world by the power of one's gaze. With the work of Kafka,

> Narration ceases to be that which presents something to be seen through the intermediary of, and from the viewpoint of, a chosen actor-spectator. The reign of circumspect consciousness—of narrative circumspection (of the "I" that looks at everything around itself and holds it by its gaze)—has been subtly shaken, without, of course, coming to an end. (*IC* 384)

Blanchot explains that Kafka "brings the neutral into play" and offers a narrative voice that no longer assumes the possibility of narrating, of telling a story (384). Instead of affirming the voice of a narrating subject, the neutral opens a space where voices disperse and the world disappears beyond the possibility of narrative to make it appear. Blanchot writes:

> The narrative "he" or "it" unseats every subject just as it disappropriates all transitive action and all objective possibility. This takes two forms: (1) the speech of the narrative always lets us feel that what is being recounted is not being recounted by anyone: it speaks in the neutral; (2) in the neutral space of the

narrative, the bearers of speech, the subjects of the action—those who once stood in the place of the characters—fall into a relation of self-nonidentification. Something happens to them that they can only recapture by relinquishing their power to say "I." (384-385)

The narrative voice would thus seem to apply both to the narrating voice and to those who speak in the narrative (which might or might not overlap, depending on the narrative perspective). In the first formulation, the narrating voice feels as if it comes from nowhere, no one. In *What is There to Say?*, Ann Smock elucidates that aspect: "Tales tend to convey this sense of an 'in back,' [Blanchot] says; a distance seems to inhabit their words and to speak in them—an outside that they don't encompass."[74] Turning to the second aspect of the narrative voice, we can also observe a sort of displacement in terms of the speaking subjects of the narrative. No longer do they speak from a place where speech is possible and where they affirm themselves as subjects through speech. Instead, the characters—a word that Blanchot abandons, at least in this passage, as a term that would appropriately describe the "subjects of the action" in the space of the neutral—become strange even to themselves and can only take shape in relation to their powerlessness to speak.

Returning to *Tropisms* with Blanchot's description of the narrative voice in mind provides a means for exploring the unsettling anonymity of the text. The first tropism in a sense announces the way that the text—the collection of tropisms—will function, even though any relation between the tropisms remains unreadable, aside from noting general thematic and stylistic similarities. The narrator of the first tropism seems to hover at the margins of the text, certainly not serving as the locus of knowledge.⁷⁵ The vague use of the pronoun "they" (does it refer to plants, people, or both?) perhaps arises not from a voice that willfully keeps us from knowing the subject of reference but from one that simply doesn't work as an identifier, a determiner, a source of light for the purposes of our clarity. At some point, though, we begin to make out the shapes of people clustering together in front of shop windows: "They looked closely at the piles of linen in the White Sale display, clever imitations of snow-covered mountains, or at a doll with teeth and eyes that, at regular intervals, lighted up, went out, lighted up, went out, lighted up, went out, each time at the same interval, lighted up again, and again went out" (13). We know very little about the anonymous groupings of people, other than the fact that they stand transfixed in front of the store displays and that their children become bored. One can note a sense of empty ritual in their outing; the narrative suggests that it's just what they do. They come out en masse from their houses to eye the product displays and to experience, in this case, the mechanical rhythms of a child's doll. Nothing distinguishes the people from one another, as they mirror the perfectly regular lighting up and going out of the doll. In Valerie Minogue's book, *Nathalie Sarraute and the War of the Words*, she describes the stylistic importance of the above passage: "The words relating to the doll, in paragraph 3, do not *describe* repetition, but exemplify it. The reader does not learn things *about* repetition and regularity, he experiences them, with the same wondering bafflement and fascination as the writer and the staring, hypnotized bystanders."⁷⁶ If the crowd's experience of the doll blinking on and off represents the pivotal moment of the first tropism, then, as Minogue suggests, it would seem that Sarraute would like to create for us that same experience by way of language. Rather than providing a narrative voice that situates us in the text with identifiable characters and a unified perspective, Sarraute provides one that lets us experience the very condition of anonymity and distraction that pervades the lives of the barely distinguishable characters who recede into the background of each tropism.

In order to explore that idea further, we can turn to the one tropism that has a named character. The eighteenth tropism exemplifies the way that Sarraute brings our attention to the surface play of the text by emphasizing linguistic and phonetic texture, sound, and self-reflexivity. Writing, like the surface-level, often banal events and conversations of the text, provides a slick surface that the reader necessarily skims across—even if that surface in some ways evokes a space beneath or outside of the world that the characters experience in a concrete way.[77] As the eighteenth tropism begins, we read, "Down below, the cook, Ada, is cleaning vegetables at a table covered in a white oilcloth. Her face is motionless, she appears to be thinking of nothing" (45). The cook's name, Ada, is a palindrome, and thus perfectly self-reflexive; in this way, the name only refers to itself, in a symmetrical and transparent way, suggesting nothing more than its own structure. In *Narcissistic Narrative*, Linda Hutcheon explains this use of language: "The linguistic self-reflexiveness or even self-generation of the text are forms of resistance to the act of reading, shifting attention to the semantic, syntactic, and often also phonetic texture of the words which actually serve to structure as well as constitute the work."[78] Hutcheon notes that self-reflexive language not only emphasizes the texture of words, but also serves to challenge the way we might want to read the text. "Ada" only signifies itself, and in this way, seemingly refuses the reading of any other signification into the word. Furthermore, Sarraute emphasizes the self-reflexivity of the name with her description of Ada, who bears no facial expression and apparently thinks of nothing—Ada certainly does not emerge as a character who invites any additional interpretation. What can we say about such a character, except that she does not seem to show any trace of *depth*? Sarraute brings our attention to Ada by uncharacteristically naming her, but then shows that a name is simply a name and only reflects itself. From the perspective that names identify individuals, we might conclude that the only named character in the text becomes as anonymous as the others and disappears into the background of a very short tropism—one that eventually shifts its attention from Ada to a woman sitting outside of a cottage. The name's significance would seem to reside in the way that it points to the surface play of the text and brings our awareness to the structure, the movement, and, sometimes, the sound of the words on the page.

Continuing with the eighteenth tropism, the original French text of the citation above reads, "La cuisinière Ada, en bas, devant la table couverte de toile cirée blanche épulche les legumes."[79] Reading the French aloud brings one's attention to the assonance of the "a" sound surrounding, and found in, Ada's name; the repetition of a certain sound not only invites us to focus on the words as phonemes, but also places emphasis on whatever may be evoked by this sound. The "a" is an open, warm sound that perhaps resonates with Ada's surroundings in an English cottage on a sunny, quiet day. We also see repetition of phrases and images throughout the tropism: "un chat est assis tout droit" and "Elle [une demoiselle] est assise là, toute raide, toute digne"; "on va sonner la cloche pour le thé" and "il sera temps [. . .] de sonner la cloche pour le thé." [80] In a tropism of less than a full page, these repetitions feel very deliberate. The repetition certainly plays upon sound and rhythm, but it also evokes a sort of infinite speech that repeats itself in every form and every phrase. Each repeated image or phrase is both the same and different from the one that precedes it. Blanchot touches upon this idea in *The Infinite Conversation* when he comments upon Gertrude Stein's famous line "a rose is a rose is a rose is a rose"; the rose is apparently nothing but itself, yet despite this sort of linguistic "purism," the repetition of the word seems to make it impossible to locate the original (whatever this original might be—word, image, object). And interestingly enough, it is from this angle that he briefly comments upon the work of Sarraute. Blanchot believes that "the secret force of certain of Nathalie Sarraute's works resides here in the enigmatic space of repetition" (*IC* 343). He writes, "*Tropisms* was already a model of this discontinuous, brief and infinite speech, the speech of thoughts that are not developed, and nonetheless more suited than any other to making us enter through interruption, and at the same time through repetition this movement of the interminable that comes to be heard beneath all literature" (343-344). Sarraute's repetition of phrases, images, "she," and "he" often gives one the impression that the narrative is continually starting over, perhaps reinitiating a conversation or thought that for some reason couldn't be finished, and re-hashing the same points that will always lead to the same place. Those aspects of narrative that traditionally allow us to distinguish one story from the next remain virtually absent; and the sense of repetition thus seeps beyond the particular words and sounds of a tropism and makes us feel that we might be reading the same tropism again and again, in slightly varied forms.

The narrative voice hovers at the surface of the text, sometimes making a brief foray into the internal world of a subject, but rarely providing much insight beyond revealing vague anxieties and hesitant reflections. Again, the narrative voice does not serve in *Tropisms* as a source of knowledge or vision, but disappears into the background, speaking from the distance of a place-less, subject-less perspective. Yet Sarraute's text often brings our attention to the insight that we might like to have, as readers, through the narrative perspective, by making us aware of the narrative voice's limitations. Our experience of that limit, of the boundaries that refuse our entrance *into* the text, focuses us on the work's slipping away from our grasp. Sometimes the sense of limitation arising in the narrative voice results from the particular narrative perspective in a tropism, and sometimes the narrator's exclusion from the "depths" or "mysteries" of the characters seems to become part of the story in a particular tropism (to the extent that we can speak of an actual narrator in the text). The tenth tropism plays with the latter scenario, as the narrator describes a group of women who routinely have tea together, gossiping about other people and mulling over decisions such as whether or not to purchase a certain outfit. The tropism begins with what seems to be a sense of narrative irony, as we read, "And what an extraordinary life it was!" in reference to "the life that women lead"—a life consisting in choosing pastries, shopping, and endlessly chatting over tea (38). Yet, rather than reading this line as a subtle critique of a bourgeois lifestyle, I think it makes more sense to consider it in conjunction with the introductory lines of the next two paragraphs:

"Tout autour c'était une volière pépiante" and "Il y avait autour d'elles un courant d'excitation."[81] With the repetition of the word "autour," the narrator emphasizes the surrounding atmosphere that hovers around the group of women, as she captures portions of the gossip and takes in appearances. The women are "pressed close together around their little tables," solidifying the boundary that separates their clique from everyone and everything else (*TP* 38). The narrator observes from outside the circle and remains a part of the exterior, overlooking space—clearly, from this vantage point, the image of "the life that women lead" seems extraordinary indeed. Returning to the first paragraph, if this does indeed exemplify narrative irony, it likely refers not to the question of whether or not such a lifestyle is extraordinary, but rather, to what one can actually perceive, especially from an exterior view, from superficial social interactions. The women—to whom the narrator always refers as "they," never individualizing them—create an impenetrable surface, both within and at the level of the narrative. As the tropism continues, we read, "Their faces seemed to be stiff with a sort of inner tension, their indifferent eyes skimmed lightly over the aspect, the mask of things, weighed it for a short second (was it pretty or ugly?) then let it drop. And their make-up gave them a hard brilliancy, a lifeless freshness" (38-39). The women's faces are tense, indifferent, and brilliant with make-up; unlike we saw with the description of Ada, though, the narrator's description communicates the possibility of depth to the reader—without, of course, revealing what that depth is. We experience the potential for depth, for insight, by way of suggestion and exclusion. The subjects in this tropism never become more than an anonymous mass of women, and they never appear to us in the way we might like to see them; the narrative voice remains in the background, outside of any definitive perspective that might provide more insight.

The ninth tropism demonstrates the way that the choice of narrative perspective can present barriers to our penetration of the text. In this particular case, the narrator provides a glimpse into one of the characters, but that insight again brings us up against a limit. The narrator begins with an opening description:

> She was sitting crouched on a corner of a chair, squirming, her neck outstretched, her eyes bulging: "Yes, yes, yes, yes," she said, and she confirmed each part of her sentence with a jerk of her head. She was frightening, mild and flat, quite smooth, and only her eyes were bulging. There was something distressing, disquieting about her and her mildness was threatening. (35)

The description leaves little doubt that the woman *is* thinking of something, or perhaps more accurately, is disturbed by something. The repetition of the word "yes," along with the nodding of her head, creates a sense of complete affirmation—yet what does she affirm? The bulging of her eyes render her sickly, or even deathly, as her ghostly figure evokes the seriousness of the situation, whatever it may be. The other character in the tropism, the man, confirms this feeling, as he fears that she might "speak, make a move, show her real self, let it come out, let it finally explode" (35-36). At the same time that we detect a certain depth of character—something unspoken, hidden, underground, appears to torment the woman—the narrator describes the woman as flat and smooth. We can note the slickness of her surface—a surface that by the end of the tropism will not have been penetrated. The man decides to leave the surface unpenetrated, the secret hidden; he does not ask any questions which would force the woman to respond, but rather, begins to "talk, talk without stopping, about just anybody, just any thing, tossing from side to side" (36). The man saves himself with words, "meaningless" words, which ceaselessly serve to fill the space between himself and the woman—in order avoid the possibility of a more meaningful exchange. Words, interestingly, provide a means to stay at the surface of the situation. But the man sees his refuge in the pointless chatter as a weakness; he perceives the possibility of confronting the depth behind the bulging eyes of the woman, but excuses himself by contending that "only someone endowed with superhuman strength would be able to do it, someone who would have the nerve to remain there opposite her, comfortably seated, well-settled in another chair, who would dare to look her calmly in the face, catch her eye, not divert his own from her squirming" (30). We see that penetrating the depth, here, does not depend upon conversation, but upon stillness, vigilance, and silence; his empty words react to his fear of this terrifying blankness.

Returning to the narrative voice, we note that the perspective functions through the thoughts and actions of the man; once the narrator initially describes the woman and suggests that there is something to be discovered or revealed, she leaves the woman sitting on the chair with nothing to say, or even to think. The reader perceives the man's fears and has insight into the threatening woman only by way of his elusive chatter; for this reason, his use of words to avoid communication also prohibits the reader's understanding, leaving the woman's depth merely suggested, rather than revealed. Because of the narrator's focalization, the man seems to provide the only possibility for revelation, but he flees from this opportunity and mindlessly talks to fill the space—in other words, the narrator invests the narrative in a man who wants to know nothing. Therefore, on two levels, the narrative refuses entrance into the text: the third-person narrator limits her perspective to that of the man, and this man prefers ignorance. Again, the narrative perspective functions in a way that leaves the characters anonymous and keeps the reader on the outside, experiencing the tension of a conversation that insists upon staying at the surface.

One other aspect of the narrative voice in *Tropisms* that preserves a sense of placelessness and anonymity concerns the way that perspective sometimes shifts in the middle of a tropism. Rather than announcing a shift in perspective, the narrative voice seems to float in and out of the internal worlds of the characters (at those times when we do have some sort of access), and also back and forth between a distanced, third-person narrator and a focalized narrator who presents the narrative from a particular perspective.[82] The eighth tropism demonstrates the way that Sarraute plays with a wandering narrative voice, as it begins with the perspective of an older man, moves through a passage in an objective third-person voice which takes us out of the man's perspective, and then concludes by engaging the perspective of the older man's grandson. And, even before the perspective shifts take place, the beginning of the tropism presents the initial subject, the older man, in terms that mislead us into identifying him as an oppressive lover, or even a sexual predator: "When he was with fresh, young creatures, innocent creatures, he felt an aching irresistible need to manipulate them with his uneasy fingers, to feel them, to bring them as close as possible, to appropriate them for himself" (32). We soon learn that these feelings belong to a grandfather taking his young grandson for a walk, which likely changes the way we read the passage. Since the rest of the tropism addresses the nature of the grandfather's desire for manipulation and appropriation in non-sexual terms, we might conclude that the language of the opening passage works to create an implicit comparison between the grandfather's behavior and that of an abusive lover. Regardless, as we are introduced to the perspective of the grandfather at the beginning of the tropism, we find ourselves confused about his basic identity, probably misidentifying the grandfather and his situation before we have a better understanding of what's going on. In *Nathalie Sarraute and the War of the Words*, Minogue points out that the narrative perspective in this tropism subtly changes, even as it continues to focus on the grandfather: "The narrative mode draws closer and closer to the old man, approximating the *discours indirect libre* [free indirect speech], as the style is steadily infiltrated by the possessive and self-justifying tics of the old man's story."[83] In other words, the narrative voice becomes even more tied to the grandfather as the tropism develops, providing us a sense for how he understands and justifies his seemingly dark and manipulative impulses towards children. This becomes apparent when reading what are, from his view, lovingly protective admonitions to the child "to look carefully, carefully, carefully, above all very carefully, when crossing the streets between the lines [. . .]" (*TP* 32).

The lesson on the dangers of crossing the street is accompanied by a more general lecture on mortality: "'What will you say when you won't have any more grandfather, he'll be gone, your grandfather will, because he's old, you know, it will soon be time for him to die. Do you know what people do when they die?'" (33). The grandfather now speaks directly to the boy, although we certainly do not have the sense that they converse; on the contrary, the inclusion of the grandfather's direct speech into the narrative marks the moment when he turns almost completely inward, revealing what appear to be his own fears. And then the grandfather disappears from the scene as a thinking, speaking subject. We read, "The air was still and gray, odorless, and the houses rose up on either side of the street, the flat masses of the houses, closed and dreary, surrounded them as they proceeded slowly along the pavement, hand in hand" (33). The narrative voice recedes into the background, leaving the grandfather and providing, from a subject-less point of view, a stark description of a stagnant, colorless, odorless, flat environment. At this moment we have the sense that the figures could be any grandfather and grandson in any town, taking a walk that in this light feels lifeless and monotonous. That tone helps us into the young boy's perspective as he struggles to take on the weight of his grandfather's oppressive presence. The boy perceives "A soft choking mass that somebody relentlessly made him take, by exerting upon him a gentle, firm pressure, by pinching his nose a bit to make him swallow it, without his being able to resist" (33). Here, we have the other side of the dynamic introduced at the very beginning of the tropism—a dynamic that takes shape by means of the shift in perspective: while the grandfather appropriates and manipulates, the helpless grandson is pried open and made to take his "medicine." Despite the grandson's sense of discomfort, he understands his role as a "good little boy, obediently holding out his little hand" (33). And despite the suggestion of much larger concerns than crossing the street, the final lines of the tropism reduce the interaction between grandfather and grandson precisely to that. The boy, in his obedience, understands that "he should always proceed cautiously and look well, first to the right, then to the left, and be careful, very careful, for fear of an accident when crossing between the lines" (34). The repetition of the language we saw from the grandfather's perspective ensures that the boy has indeed ingested the lessons from the walk. Interestingly, although we have shifted perspective in terms of the narrative voice, the figures of the grandfather and grandson merge into one another; the grandfather's desire to appropriate the boy leads to the boy's appropriation of the grandfather's perspective, as he repeats almost verbatim the grandfather's teachings and justifications for his oppressive behavior.

Even though the grandfather certainly introduces weighty topics into the one-sided conversation with his grandson in the eighth tropism, those topics linger rather than becoming the subject of a serious conversation (after all, the grandson is still at an age where he learns to look both ways to cross the street). Most conversations in *Tropisms* remain at the level of insignificant chatter, due to, for example, fear or social convention, and that chatter dominates the interactions of the speaking subjects throughout the text. While the narrative voice tends to provide the sense that we are skimming the surface of these conversations, experiencing each tropism by means of what the movements and sound of the language may offer, the anonymous, almost shapeless characters and their interactions perhaps reveal something "more," precisely by way of their general refusal to interact in a more overtly meaningful way. That takes us to Sarraute's notion of tropism, an idea that ends up playing an important role throughout her oeuvre. In a forward to *Tropisms*, Sarraute describes:

> These movements, of which we are hardly cognizant, slip through us on the frontiers of consciousness in the form of undefinable, extremely rapid sensations. They hide behind

our gestures, beneath the words we speak and the feelings we manifest, all of which we are aware of experiencing, and are able to define. They seemed, and still seem to me to constitute the secret source of our existence, in what might be called its nascent state. (6)

Sarraute therefore distinguishes these movements—tropisms—from outward, recognizable experiences that are often manifested by individuals. The fleeting nature of the tropisms makes them impossible to express with words—at the level of conversation or narrative—and they are thus only suggested by way of the commonplace events and interactions that in some ways seem to oppose or hide them. Therefore, the most banal conversations and actions in *Tropisms* become a means for investigating the practically unnoticeable "rapid sensations" that, for Sarraute, constitute a sort of primordial foundation for human experience—one that we barely sense and cannot express. Sarraute continues:

> The dramatic situations constituted by these invisible actions interested me as such. Nothing could distract my attention from them and nothing should distract that of the reader; neither the personality of the characters or the plot, by means of which ordinarily, the characters evolve. The barely visible, anonymous character was to serve as a mere prop for these movements, which are inherent in everybody and can take place in anybody, at any moment. (8)

Here, we have Sarraute's explanation for the anonymity of her characters; it would seem that characters not only threaten to get in the way of the movements, but they also contradict the nature of those movements by suggesting individuality rather than universality. In other words, traditional character development creates individuals, whereas Sarraute shifts focus to the invisible movements that underlie all individuals. The character becomes unimportant from this perspective, as "he" or "she" could be anyone. Yet "he" and "she," in their awkward, often anxiety-ridden exchanges, also serve as "props"—unimportant and imperfect, but necessary—for the movements that interest Sarraute.

In a preface that Jean-Paul Sartre wrote to Sarraute's first novel, *Portrait of a Man Unknown*, he focuses on the distinction between "authentic" and "inauthentic" conversation when discussing Sarraute's work. He makes reference to Heidegger's concept of "they" talk—as Blanchot does in his essay on Louis-René des Forêts's *The Bavard*—in order to identify the various commonplace, surface-level conversations exchanged between nearly all of the characters in *Tropisms*. Sartre writes:

> Nathalie Sarraute shows us the wall of inauthenticity rising on every side. But what is behind this wall? As it happens, there's nothing, or rather almost nothing. Vague attempts to flee something whose lurking presence we sense dimly. *Authenticity*, that is, the real connection with others, with oneself and with death, is suggested at every turn, although remaining invisible. We feel it because we flee it.[84]

Sartre recognizes the way that conversation becomes a means of avoiding and preventing the threat of connection quietly and invisibly underlying the interactions throughout *Tropisms*. As noted in the ninth tropism, the man chatters away, hoping that his incessant flow of words will prevent the obviously troubled woman with whom he interacts to refrain from revealing herself, her feelings. Sartre's conceptualization of the "lurking presence" beneath the superficial conversation becomes problematic, though, when we consider the way he seems to privilege the individual in his description of *authenticity*. Sartre, perhaps as a result of bringing his own philosophical perspective to his reading of Sarraute, has missed what I believe Sarraute characterizes as a space of even more profound anonymity. The speaking subjects of *Tropisms* live and interact in an anonymous space—"he" and "she" repeat the same motions, have the same pointless conversations, and simultaneously get trapped and find refuge in the conventions of everyday life. But that anonymity conceals the even less shapeless and subject-less space of the invisible movements "which are inherent in everybody and can take place in anybody, at any moment" (*TP* 8). As Ann Jefferson explains in *Nathalie Sarraute, Fiction and Theory*, "The inner life may be opposed to the external world of social and physical existence, but it is one where differences of all kinds are thoroughly erased. The psychology of the *tropism* is one that presupposes that differences, even if they exist, do not count."[85] The realm of social convention and "inauthentic" babble in *Tropisms* certainly suggests a lack of individuality due to the monotony of everyday routines, the fear of intimacy, the inability to express oneself, and the pressure to conform; but Sarraute radicalizes, rather than opposes, the anonymity of that realm by proposing one where we disappear into an undifferentiated mass of invisible movements—"the secret source of our existence, in what might be called its nascent state" (*TP* 6).

Sarraute's notion of tropism can take us a in a variety of directions within and away from the text, but I would like to maintain focus on the way that the question of anonymity reflects the space of the neutral. The underlying realm of tropisms that Sarraute proposes compounds the sense of anonymity that the subjects in her text experience in their everyday lives. That underground space, to which the subjects have practically no access, seems to provide an abyss rather than a foundation concerning the possibility of establishing individuality. Rather than existing as a theoretical space where the subjects might come into relation with their "authentic selves," the tropistic realm offers the possibility of an even more profound disappearance where the mass of underground movements dominates and individuals matter not. As noted earlier, Blanchot mentions that "in the neutral space of the narrative, the bearers of speech, the subjects of the action—those who once stood in the place of the characters—fall into a relation of self-nonidentification. Something happens to them that they can only recapture by relinquishing their power to say 'I'" (*IC* 384-385). Those characteristics parallel what we saw with the narrative voice—a voice that wanders, no longer speaking from a single, privileged perspective that serves to illuminate. The subjects of the action in *Tropisms* struggle to assert themselves, to communicate, to establish subjectivity, and to deal with the subjectivity of others. From that perspective, the subjects continually recede into the backgrounds of their environments, disappearing as a result of the apparent powerlessness to individuate themselves. Not only do the subjects lack names, but they also continually find themselves in situations where they feel like strangers to themselves and to other people.

Turning more specifically to the conversations where we can see the subjects confront their anonymity—at both the level of social convention and the underground movement of tropisms—we can often note the inability of the speakers to avoid returning again and again to the same clichés and banalities, not knowing what else to say. The fourth tropism begins: "They were jabbering half-expressed things, with a far off look as though they were following inwardly some subtle, delicate sentiment that they seemed unable to convey" (21). Here, we have another situation where two subjects converse with one another in a way that appears to hide the very thing that drives the discussion. The language in this passage emphasizes the inability of the subjects to express a feeling of which they are aware, and points to their powerlessness to do anything other than "jabber." Interestingly, although the subjects find themselves unable to communicate with one another about the "subtle, delicate sentiment," they both seem to sense the same thing; in other words, the sentiment looms beneath the speech of each subject but is not unique to either one. In some sense, the direct expression of the sentiment would seem unnecessary, except that its suppression clearly causes tension and suggests that the actual speaking of the sentiment greatly differs from simply feeling it in an unspoken way. The subjects serve as "props" for the sentiment—remember Sarraute's own language in *The Age of Suspicion*—and bring it to life by "playing a game" (20). The narrative emphasizes the dance-like and theatrical nature of the conversation by which the subjects both manifest and hide the unspoken sentiment. "There, there, there, they danced, pirouetted and wheeled about, providing a little wit, a little intelligence, but as though without touching anything, without ever moving on to the forbidden plane that might displease him" (20). The language dances like the two subjects, turning on the repetition of "there," and detailing each step in the complicated interaction. Turning briefly to the essay, "Conversation and Sub-Conversation," Sarraute discusses the way that the performative, game-like elements of conversation articulate with the unspoken "sub-conversation":

> Here the inner movements, of which the dialogue is merely the outcome and as it were the furthermost point—usually prudently tipped to allow it to come up to the surface—try to extend their action into the dialogue itself. To resist their constant pressure and contain them, the conversation stiffens, becomes stilted, it adopts a cautious, slackened pace. But it is because of this pressure that it stretches and twists into long sinuous sentences. Now a close, subtle game, which is also a savage game, takes place between the conversation and the sub-conversation.
>
> More often than not, the inside gets the better of it: something keeps cropping out, becoming manifest, disappearing then coming back again; something that continually threatens to make everything explode.[86]

Sarraute indicates a sort of back-and-forth movement as the sub-conversation pushes against the walls of the conversation that contain it. These two oppositions are at play, giving and taking, exerting pressure on one another. Despite the domination of conversation in the relationship—a domination that characterizes the interactions in *Tropisms*—Sarraute believes that the sub-conversation does not relent, and further, manages to affect the functioning of the conversation. Sartre appears to touch on this idea when analyzing Sarraute's work: "The fact is that these groping, shamefaced evasions, which seek to remain nameless, are also relationships with others. Thus the sacred conversation, the ritualistic exchange of commonplaces, hides a 'half-voiced conversation,' in which the valves touch, lick and inhale one another."[87] We might conclude that the importance of commonplace conversation lies not in the mostly empty, insignificant words, but rather, in the performance of their exchange; the ritualistic chatter brings to light the disappearance of the sub-conversation and maintains the anonymity of the powerless speaking subjects.

Returning to the fourth tropism, Sarraute's discussion of the articulation of conversation and sub-conversation clearly characterizes the back-and-forth of the two subjects and the unfolding of an increasingly tense interaction. While the conversational dance appears to maintain a lighthearted tone at first, it would seem that pressure from the unspoken sub-conversation makes the subjects aware that something is at stake in their game-playing. The narrative voice soon takes the perspective of one of the subjects—a wife, perhaps?—whose thoughts take us through the strategies and pitfalls of the particular conversation with "him." After having some success with "a naïve manner so as to dare to say truths that might seem harsh, to show interest in him," the subject mis-steps and brings up a topic of conversation that causes "him" to frown (*TP* 23). While the subject appears to enjoy the dance while it lasts, the danger of making an error looms—especially considering "how frightening he is" (23). When playing roles, one risks forgetting the lines; in *Tropisms*, that inevitability results in misunderstandings, confrontations, and anxieties. In the end, the role-playing and its results generally feel unavoidable, as they arise from the continual pressure of the unspoken and the powerlessness of the subjects to express that "subtle, delicate sentiment" beneath or outside of the actual conversations. In the space of the neutral, the subjects' relation with themselves and with others only comes about by way of their inability to assert themselves as subjects, to say "I," to say anything at all.

In the second tropism, we have a subject who specifically reflects on the nature of commonplace conversation and his inability to escape its grasp. In the beginning of the tropism, a woman and her cook talk about the visitors to the house, gossiping about their families and criticizing their lifestyles: "'And that daughter of theirs, she's not married yet, and she's not bad, she has pretty hair, her nose is small, and her feet are pretty too.'—'Yes, pretty hair, that's true,' she said, 'but, you know, nobody likes her, she's not attractive. It's really funny'" (16). From another room, "he" (perhaps the woman's son?) hears the chatter of the two women, and "their thought filtered into him, lined him internally" (16). In the case of this tropism, the conversation of the two women clearly conveys a sense of pettiness and focuses on appearances and social expectations. Unlike some of the other tropisms, these women don't seem particularly struck by the fact that their conversations are limited to "shallow" concerns and clichés. But the conversation penetrates, "filters" into, the male subject who lies within its reach. The narrative perspective shifts to the male subject as soon as he is introduced, and he focuses on the sort of thought that inspires the conversation of the women: "And he sensed percolating from the kitchen, humble, squalid, time-marking human thought, marking time in one spot, always in one spot, going round and round, in circles, as if they were dizzy but couldn't stop [. . .]" (16). As the language mimes the circularity it describes, it also creates the sense that, at least from the male subject's perspective, such conversations and ways of thinking become inescapable for those who become trapped in them. And, beyond that, the thought "filters" into him, into his life; "[t]o avoid it was impossible" (17). In *Nathalie Sarraute, Fiction and Theory*, Jefferson remarks that the description of the "squalid" thought works as a series of substitutable similes, which reinforces the feeling of habitual repetition and brings attention to the sameness of various activities that one can reduce to a single basic urge.[88] Sarraute's passage compares the thought of the women to "the way we bite our nails, the way we tear off dead skin when we're peeling, the way we scratch ourselves when we have hives, the way we toss in our beds [. . .]" (17). It would seem that even in our resistance to certain ways of thinking and conversing—the boy lies on his bed and critiques the conversation he hears, rather than participating—we have probably already participated in an equivalent activity, which, when it comes down to it, reflects our sameness with what we reject. Despite the suggestion of sameness, of a sort of anonymity that would equate the listening subject to the women conversing in the kitchen, the subject at this point allows for the possibility that all of the habits are not the same and are not inevitable; he thinks, "But perhaps for them it was something else" (17).

Momentarily giving himself an "out" and maintaining the possibility that he is not like "them," the male character continues with a series of reflections about the falsities of everyday communication: "Everywhere, in countless forms, 'deception' [. . .] everywhere, in the guise of life itself, it caught hold of you as you went by, when you hurried past the concierge's door, when you answered the telephone, lunched with the family, invited your friends, spoke a word to anybody, whoever it might be" (17).

One of the unique aspects of this tropism is that we have more insight into a subject's thinking than is typical of most of the other tropisms. In addition, this subject rejects what he sees as the deceptive nature of petty conversation and social ritual (whereas other subjects often seem to welcome the distraction and protection such forms of communication offer). At the same time, the subject pronounces his defeat almost as soon as he dismisses the "guise of life" that apparently stands in for something more honest and "real." "You had to answer them and encourage them gently, and above all, above everything, not make them feel, not make them feel a single second, that you're different. Be submissive, be submissive, be retiring [. . .]" (17). Here the repetition creates the sense that the subject must tell himself again and again to behave a particular way, to sink into the repetitive, empty motions of the "guise of life," and to disappear into the anonymity of resembling everyone else. He recognizes that not doing so would lead to "a rending, an uprooting, something unexpected, something violent would happen, something that had never happened before, and which would be frightful" (17). The subject clearly fears the result of asserting himself outside of the sameness to which he is expected to conform, as if "they," those who expect, will respond violently to his claim of difference. At this moment, then, it would seem that the anonymity of subjects—their lack of distinction as individuals—results from the social pressure to conform. But arriving at that conclusion misses a few important points that complicate the subject's unspoken desire to perform his individuality. The subject in the second tropism critiques the social habits and conversations he witnesses at the same time that he sees himself merging into the masses of people from whom he can barely distinguish himself—especially since he admits that he fulfills the expectations of empty social ritual. While he wants to assert his independence, it never becomes clear in the tropism whether or not he truly can be distinguished from the sameness that seems to haunt him. We never have a sense of his subjectivity or individuality, beyond his desire to distinguish himself from the norm and, essentially, to establish subjectivity. From that perspective, the subject's rejection of sameness reflects the way that he is not able to be anything other than the same, anything other than a subject without subjectivity. Jefferson explains that such conflict in Sarraute's work "lies in the inherent nature of subjectivity as matter that lacks shape and consistency and which therefore cannot easily be contained within limits."[89] That shapelessness recalls Blanchot's description of the subject in the space of the neutral. The subject in the second tropism struggles to define himself and his difference from others, confronting not so much the social pressures to conform but the underlying threat of disappearance that results from his powerlessness to do anything other than conform.[90]

Sarraute's *Tropisms* offers a number of paths where we can explore the complexities of a neutral space where subjects speak without the ability to do so; where the narrative voice wanders from place to place without providing a locus from which we might gain sight; where the text itself always feels as if it escapes our grasp, even as it leaves traces of the moments it recounts through the sounds and repetitions of the language. The theme of disappearance arises in these various ways, and the anonymous subjects and commonplace situations blur into one another, making it difficult to distinguish one tropistic moment from the next. As Sarraute herself notes, the word "tropism" refers to the orientation of an organism either toward or away from a stimulus, such as light. She writes, "I gave them this name because of their spontaneous, irresistible, instinctive nature, similar to that of the movements made by certain living organisms under the influence of outside stimuli, such as light or heat" (*TR* 8). She adds that the analogy refers to "the instinctive, irresistible nature of the movements, which are produced in us by the presence of others, or by objects from the outside world" (8). Interestingly, considering especially the conversations of the subjects in the text, as the light of day calls forward the underground movements, those movements become something else—something that conceals their origin and marks the impossibility of bringing them to light. In other words, each literary tropism in Sarraute's text inscribes the disappearance of the tropism that inspires it. In confrontation with the impossible demand that writing a series of tropisms seems to involve, *Tropisms* begins, unable to begin, climbing the walls and poking through the cracks of the town's structures in the first tropism.

Chapter 6: Into the Night: Blanchot's *L'arrêt de mort*

Blanchot's *récit L'arrêt de mort* explores the disappearance of the work, both at the level of the events that take place in the story and at the level of the narrator's efforts to tell that which cannot be told. The Orphic quest to retrieve Eurydice from the depths of the night takes shape again and again over the course of the narrative and also by way of the narrative. Turning to Blanchot's storytelling in his critical essays—stories about mythic encounters, resurrection, and calls into the night—provides a means for approaching *L'arrêt de mort* in that same vein. In addition to playing out Orpheus's descent into the night, the narrative resonates with the call of Jesus to the dead Lazarus: *Lazare, veni foras*. And it evokes Ulysses's encounter with the sirens, especially when considering the narrator's reflections upon the impossible task of telling the events that both inspire his narrative and remain absent from it.[91] In essence, those stories all recount and enact a similar event—a moment of impatience and decision which sends the work away at the same time that it allows for it to begin. *L'arrêt de mort* sheds light on that moment where all is lost, where the work disappears into the night where it begins.

Blanchot's narrator in *L'arrêt de mort* begins his narrative by recounting his history of failure—specifically the failure to tell the events in his life that he now intends to tell. He admits, "I have already tried to put them into writing several times. If I have written books, it has been in the hope that they would put an end to it all. If I have written novels, they have come into being just as the words began to shrink back from the truth."[92] The narrator draws a connection between the act of writing and some sort of end or death, apparently hoping that recounting the events would reveal the truth and thus "put an end to it all." We have the sense that the narrator's inability to bring the events to expression allows for their lingering presence, which is confounded by the fact that expressing them—writing them—creates distance from the truth they attempt to tell. When the narrator writes, the words "shrink back" and the truth disappears. So how does one tell the truth of a story when the telling of that story necessarily sends the truth away? There is something about the truth that makes the telling impossible, and yet there is perhaps something about the telling that puts an end to the truth precisely by missing it.

The narrator's telling of his experience becomes an endless project to which he returns again and again, apparently without finding completion to his work. Past efforts seem to indicate that recounting the truth of the events remains beyond the narrator's grasp, yet something about writing, about turning to the language of literature, convinces the narrator that he might indeed achieve closure. Blanchot's reflections on the plight of the writer in *The*

Space of Literature illuminate the perspective that the narrator of *L'arrêt de mort* offers. Blanchot writes:

> The obsession which ties [the writer] to a privileged theme, which obliges him to say over again what he has already said [. . .] illustrates the necessity, which apparently determines his efforts, that he always come back to the same point, pass again over the same paths, persevere in starting over what for him never starts, and that he belong to the shadow of events, not their reality, to the image, not the object, to what allows words themselves to become images, appearances—not signs, values, the power of truth. (*SL* 24)

The narrator of *L'arrêt de mort* emphasizes his continual reprisal of the same work, as if it just won't go away; he seems obligated to "pass again over the same paths," since he never completes, or even begins, his journey. Yet, interestingly, he appears to return to his narrative with a sense of confidence that things might be different this time: "But until now, words have been frailer and more cunning than I would have liked" (*AM* 131). The "until now" of that statement suggests that the frailty and cunning of words—that which perhaps causes them to "shrink back from the truth"—no longer presents the same problem for the narrator. What has changed? Does the narrator mean to suggest that he now bears a certain mastery of words that allows him to reveal the truth that has until now eluded him? Such an interpretation does not account for the narrator's continued skepticism throughout the *récit* concerning the ability of the narrative to capture the truth. Rather, the narrator shifts our attention away from the words and the narrative itself as the locus of truth, provoking us to search elsewhere. In his discussion of *L'arrêt de mort* in *Versions of Pygmalion*, J. Hillis Miller writes,

"[The narrator] insinuates repeatedly that the truth is to be found not in the words but between them or outside them, perhaps outside the borders of the *récit* altogether."[93] It would seem that the narrator recognizes that his writing belongs to the shadow of events, that "shrinking back" represents the most salient function of his medium. After all, he tells us at the end of the first section of the text that "What is extraordinary begins at the moment I stop" (*AM* 151).

After resolving to recommence his narrative, perhaps on different terms, the narrator announces, "I will write freely, since I am sure that this story concerns no one but myself" (131). That comment makes us aware of our apparently unimportant role, as readers, in the coming about of the narrative—at least, as far as it concerns the narrator's purpose. The narrator's desire to recount certain events in his life has nothing to do with making some sort of revelation, through writing, to the reader (which would presumably be impossible anyways, given what he suggests about the way that words hide, or shrink back, from the truth). The narrator's comment thus provokes us to ask ourselves what compels him to write an account of his experiences, if they only concern him. One way to view his narrative involves considering it as a reprisal of his experiences with J. and Nathalie—even if that means being turned away at the essential moment, suffering exclusion in the most agonizing way. In other words, the narrator may reinitiate his nocturnal descent by way of writing, taking him towards the impossible point where both he and the work disappear, where he again loses everything at the moment his impatient gaze ruins the journey. That re-opening of the depths, by beginning again what he can't possibly begin, aligns the writing of his narrative with the events his narrative will tell. The narrator's work, his writing, re-enacts the resurrection of J., solicits the deathly stare of Nathalie, evokes the numerous irrational intrusions into dark apartments, and brings about his own deathly illness. The story *is* the event that it tells and re-tells, and it depends on its own disappearance into the night in order to begin.

As the narrator hesitantly begins to recount the situation surrounding his relationship with J. and the events of her illness, it's hard to miss the collection of specific dates identifying, non-chronologically, various moments that relate in one way or another to the over-arching story: the principal events of the narrative took place in 1938; the narrator is telling them nine years later on October 8th; someone almost discovered "proof" of the events in 1940; something important happened on October 13th of 1938; the narrator went to Paris in early September of that year; J., despite her condition, took car-rides outdoors until the 5th or 6th of October. All of those dates appear within the first several paragraphs of the narrative and end up feeling simultaneously vague and awkwardly specific. The narrator seems to go to great lengths to establish a sort of timeline, promising that "The principal dates should be found in a little notebook in my desk," but soon after admits that such information is "hardly important" (133). And the narrator's continual, choppy movements backward and forward in time make the timeline more confusing than helpful, especially since certain important details are left conspicuously unidentified. Regardless, the narrator attempts to situate the story in specific places and times, as if that might be the only way to establish a sort of groundwork for the strangeness—perhaps placelessness and timelessness—of the events he begins to tell. In addition, as the narrative takes shape and some of the details become marginally clearer, the timeline, as a sort of linear configuration, makes less and less sense. In other words, we have more dates and details but also more blurring and confusion about the relationship of specific markers in the chronology of the story. It would seem from the start that the narrator is trying, if half-heartedly, to make concrete something that remains elusive.

The narrator then begins to describe J.'s illness, focusing on the last weeks of her life, which he actually does not directly witness because of a job assignment in Arcachon. In "Living On," Jacques Derrida notes the repetition of the prefix *tele-* in *L'arrêt de mort* as a way to suggest the significance of the interval separating the narrator from J. throughout the narrative.[94] He notes that the narrator communicates with J. and her caregivers by *tele*phone and *tele*gram; I would also add that, due to his geographical distance from J.'s deathbed, he often learns of her condition through secondary sources—a doctor who does not inspire very much confidence with his inaccurate diagnoses and a sister who does not "have much presence of mind, nor much heart" (*AM* 144). J. writes letters in tortured, illegible handwriting, eventually dictates her letters through a friend, and suffers coughing attacks when trying to serve as her own voice. All of those conditions point to a certain distance that leaves the narrator infinitely outside of J. and her experience, and even he fails to understand why he chooses to maintain this separation. He remarks:

> Today I try without success to understand why I stayed away from Paris then, when everything was calling me back. The thought of that absence makes me uneasy, yet the reasons for it escape me. Mysterious as were the consequences of those

events, it seems to me that my deliberate absence, which allowed them to happen, is even more mysterious. (138)

It seems that the narrator instinctively perceives the importance and necessity of his distance, even if he doesn't know why. He believes the interval to be deliberate, yet irrational, and also credits it with providing a space for the miraculous events that eventually take place. After all, it is the narrator, following his apparent neglect of J. during her last days and hours of life, who calls her back to life; he comes late to the moment of her death, yet has the power to resurrect her. The narrator knows very well that J. is dying, but it seems that he must remain distant in order not to risk losing her in the way he wants her. In other words, the narrator wants J. *as distance*, to the degree that that distance represents her closeness with death. If we see this in terms of Orpheus's descent towards Eurydice, we might imagine that collapsing the distance would only allow the narrator to retrieve J. from her relation with death and bring her into the world of living, speaking beings. Like Orpheus, the narrator appears to seek J. in her deathly state, even as she disappears beyond his grasp.

As the narrator recalls times he shared with J. throughout her illness, he reveals a curious interest in preserving her existence in various ways. He makes vague mention of mysterious objects hidden in closets and secret notes that he never discloses, but there are also other vestiges about which he speaks openly. Interestingly, these relics of J. all focus on capturing her deathly state, rather than providing a certain proof of her vivacity, or life. The narrator hangs onto a cast of her hands that reveals her lifeline, he mentions a photograph that shows her bulging eyes, "pushed from their sockets by the fever," he still keeps a copy of the depressing will she wrote that purposely excludes him, and he tells of his request to embalm her body (133). The narrator seems especially drawn to the traces of J. that show her proximity to death; that preoccupation supports the notion that his fascination with the dying woman revolves precisely around the dying, the sickliness, the ghostly appearance, the coming disappearance. His first description of J. notes that "without make-up she seemed even younger, she was almost too young, so that the main effect of the disease was to give her the features of an adolescent. Only her eyes, which were larger, blacker, and more brilliant than they should have been [. . .] had an abnormal fixity" (133). While J.'s illness makes her look younger, it also renders her "too young" and makes her eyes appear other than they "should" be. J.'s youthful appearance and striking eyes demonstrate that she seems already to have gone *beyond* natural limits. In addition to her facial features, J.'s hands bear an inscription—a "deep hatchet-stroke" running the length of the palm—that suggests her intimacy with dying and her defiant struggle to confront it, even to surpass it. The narrator suggests that J. have a cast of her hands made and then sends it off to a professional palm reader, who examines the cast and, despite the line, surprisingly comes to the conclusion that ""[J.] will not die"" (137-138). That prediction seems strange, seeing as it is perhaps the only prediction that would appear to have no chance of being fulfilled. Yet, this paradox, J.'s closeness with death, her courage simultaneously to penetrate it and deny it, to surrender to it and surpass it, fascinates the narrator *and* keeps him at a distance. He cherishes the relics that remind him not of her, but of her relation with death. Again, his Orphic quest does not simply seek to preserve J. as a living figure, but to resurrect her in death—just as

Orpheus does not desire the recognizable Eurydice of the day, but rather, the Eurydice of the night.

While the narrator tells of his pursuit of J. from a distance and his efforts to keep tabs on her movement deeper and deeper into the night, he also recalls their first encounter when J. plays the more active role and inexplicably enters his room in the middle of the night. She calls to the narrator through the door of his hotel room, frightened that he is dying, and he responds, "Don't be afraid" (135). The narrator notes the seeming humor of this strange first interaction with J., but insists that "the impulse which carried her towards an unknown man in the middle of the night, which left her at his mercy, was a noble impulse, and she acted on it in the most true and just manner" (135). Something draws J. into the night, towards the man she believes to be dying; she calls out, and he responds "in a strange voice, more frightening than reassuring" (135). In a sense, J. has taken on the Orphic role in this scene, intruding into a forbidden, tomb-like space in order to call the narrator back from the depths of the night. The narrator responds in a voice that is not his own—he is apparently still sleeping—and awakens to find J. in his room. That penetration of the night initiates the narrator's relationship with J. and provides the foundation for their strange, distant interaction over the course of the next couple years—even if the narrator generally pursues the dying J. into the night, rather than the reversal of that dynamic represented in their first encounter. J.'s entrance into the narrator's room also seems to set the stage for repeated instances of the same scene throughout both parts of the narrative—not only between J. and the narrator, but also involving Colette, Simone, and Nathalie. One person lies in wait in the blackness of an enclosed, private space, and another fearfully enters that space, calling the stranger from the night and establishing an Orphic relation. The continual role reversal—sometimes the narrator plays the intruder and sometimes he listens for the distant call through his closed door—emphasizes the repetition of this scene in variations. Each character in the narrative hovers close to death *and* calls others back from death. Cast in such a manner, no oppositional relation between the characters is stable. Although the narrator, both as writer and resurrector of J., often fulfills the Orphic role of the one who descends towards an inaccessible death, his own proximity to death and disappearance—to the infinite recession beyond the grasp of a pursuer—causes a blurring of the defined roles. J. initiates the relationship with the narrator as Orpheus only in order to hand it off, to switch roles. The narrator arises out of his own deathbed to take on that role and pursue J. towards the space from whence he came. In this way, a sort of circularity is established where the many similar, yet seemingly distinct, relationships get caught up. It seems that the circularity of recession, pursuit, and resurrection allows for substitutions—the movement infinitely repeats itself, but the players exchange roles.

In spite of the repetitions of the Orphic quest that seem to involve all of the characters, J.'s movement towards death and her subsequent resurrection remains the most striking and literal example of a sort of play at the limit of life and death, appearance and disappearance. Several times throughout her illness, J.'s doctor pronounces her "death sentence," giving her a certain amount of time to live before the disease takes her life. The narrator explains, "Her doctor had told me that from 1936 on he had considered her dead" (134). In that way, J.'s life, at least according to the doctor, appears to exceed, or surpass, what should have already been her last days; she triumphs over the disease by outliving the expectations for her death. It becomes a life on top of, or beyond, the *natural* limits of her life. The *arrêt de mort*, from this point of view, can refer both to the sentence imposed by the doctor that attempts to determine the moment of death, and to the seeming suspension of this death—living beyond the death sentence. Of course, the suspension of death, or living on of life, becomes further complicated when J. does indeed die before coming back to life. That resurrection therefore implies a living beyond of a life that was already living beyond its notional limitations. In "Living On," Derrida refers to Blanchot's *The Step Not Beyond*, where Blanchot describes *living on* as a movement of supplementarity that suspends both life and death. Derrida explains the paradoxical, double suspension in the following fashion:

> This enduring, lasting, going on, stresses or insists *on* the "on" of a living on that bears the entire enigma of this supplementary logic. Survival and *revenance*, living on and returning from the dead: living on goes beyond both living and dying, supplementing each with a sudden surge and a certain reprieve, deciding [*arrêtant*] life *and* death, ending them in a decisive *arrêt*, the *arrêt* that puts an end to something and the *arrêt* that condemns with a sentence [*sentence*], a statement, a spoken word or a word that goes on speaking.[95]

Living on, whether it refers to the surpassing of a death sentence or the resurrection from the decision of death, supplements both life and death, at the same time that it decisively opens them up to a moment of infinite indecision. Blanchot's text plays in that moment, in that space, which lacks foundation and definition—it is the in between, the *entretien*, interrupting and connecting life and death, living and living on, the calling forth and the response, the descent and the recession, writing and its disappearance.

In the midst of J.'s illness, the narrator observes and admires "her cold and watchful look in the face of death" (*AM* 134). She has reached a point where the life-draining characteristics of her illness bring her to a paradoxical moment in her fight to survive. The narrator explains that "now she cursed both the disease and life itself with all the violence she could rouse" (133). While the narrator wonders whether J. wants to live or die, it would seem that she rejects both living and dying, as surrendering to either would equate to choosing the better of two evils. Fighting for life would in a sense affirm the value of a life that has offered pain and cruelty, whereas fighting for death would imply surrendering herself to the ravages of an unjust disease. In other words, J. wants neither to live nor to die, and so she curses both with violence, which demonstrates the decisiveness of her refusal to choose. J. will not accept a passive role in her movement towards death, which perhaps inspires her to contemplate taking her own life. When she suggests suicide, the narrator advises it, since he has already determined her sustained life to be a reprieve from an imminent death. Suicide, following Blanchot's line of thinking in *The Space of Literature*, parallels art, or writing, since "each of these two movements is testing a singular form of *possibility*. Both involve a power that wants to be power even in the region of the ungraspable, where the domain of goals ends" (106, emphasis in original). J. demonstrates a powerful willfulness throughout her illness, apparently staving off death each day she lives on. Proposing suicide implies that J. might take that *power* to the next level, to the limit where a reversal occurs and she enters a domain of powerlessness where her constant efforts and struggle cannot accomplish anything. Blanchot explains, though, both in the case of suicide and of writing, that the empowered act of one who seeks the ultimate reversal infinitely excludes him or her from it. Neither death nor the work belongs to the realm of accomplishment; when all is made to disappear, disappearance remains. When the narrator agrees to J.'s suggestion of suicide, she confronts the already determined failure of her terrifying movement towards death—in the sense that her death will not capture her death, and any effort to take control of it will only emphasize its movement beyond her grasp. From that point of view, J.'s descent, her dying, and ultimately her death, can only paradoxically, impossibly succeed as long as she doesn't die; suicide, therefore, does not provide the solution she seeks. Moreover, the narrator's willingness to entertain J.'s suicidal plans demonstrates his awareness that death remains infinitely distant regardless of J.'s actions. In any case, the narrator perceives that neither death nor *not* dying communicates or takes power over death.

J. decides to write a will after the narrator agrees to her suicide. Since the narrator does not contest her suggestion to kill herself, she excludes him from the will, though she does not intend for him to see it. The narrator takes the will from her and describes the impression it has on him: "That tiny will, in keeping with her propertyless, already dispossessed existence, that last thought, from which I was excluded, touched me infinitely. In it I recognized her violence, her secrecy; I saw that she was at liberty to fight me even up to the last second" (134). While the mention of property and dispossession evoke the fact that J. and her family literally have nothing actually to sign over in a will, that language also suggests her state of existence while dying. Clearly, J.'s gradual disappearance as she approaches death continues to fascinate the narrator, who even seems to recognize the inevitability of his exclusion from such "deathbed" statements. Her movement towards death does not, and cannot, involve him; death necessarily remains absolutely individual and personal, though simultaneously anonymous and universal. The fact that J. excludes the narrator also emphasizes the interval that maintains their relation. As noted earlier, the narrator must, like Orpheus, remain at a patient distance in order to preserve J.'s disappearance into the depths of the night; his exclusion from the will, though not his own doing, affirms his distance. In addition, although J. authors her own will, it necessarily excludes her also, since it can only be enacted after she dies. The writing of the will interestingly evokes the relationship of death and writing; for Blanchot, the book, "a mute collection of sterile words," functions as a sort of will that announces the figurative death of the writer and his or her exclusion from the work (*SL* 23). The book only comes into being once the writer lets go of his or her approach to the work, even though its existence has depended upon, and arises out of, the writer's relationship with the work. From that point of view, J.'s will announces her death and excludes her in a way that parallels the book's pronouncement of the writer's disappearance from his or her work.

As J. becomes increasingly sick, she turns to writing in sometimes small, but significant ways—the writing of her will and of various letters, in particular. In addition, the last events and statements of her (first) death clearly evoke those of Franz Kafka, as recorded by Max Brod. Kafka, of course, serves as a central figure in Blanchot's thought about writing; the prominence of Kafka in

Blanchot's work generally concerns the way that Kafka exemplifies the plight of the writer who completely gives himself over to the approach of literature. Kafka's well-documented struggles illuminate the writer's tenuous relationship with life and literature, as both continually and necessarily exclude him. In *Bataille, Klossowski, Blanchot: Writing at the Limit*, Leslie Hill notes the references to Brod's account of Kafka's last days in J.'s behaviors, symptoms, and medications—for example, "a renewed determination to live, coupled with a genuine fear of suffering."[96] Both Kafka and J. eventually die from a double dose of the same medication, and, most significantly, J.'s threat to the doctor—"If you don't kill me, you'll kill me"—repeats verbatim Brod's quotation of Kafka's memorable deathbed statement (*AM* 141). At this point in the *récit*, J. has apparently accepted the inevitability of her impending death, and merely seeks to reduce the suffering caused both by the pain of the illness and by the slow process of dying itself. If the doctor were to refuse J. the injection that basically seals her death and calms her fight against the illness, she claims that he would kill her from prolonging her suffering and intensifying her struggle. Yet the paradoxes continue when, like Kafka, J. reacts to the dose of morphine with a "vigilance, a penetrating gaze that left her enemy no hope of attacking her unawares" (141). Thus, the medication that supposedly encourages calmness, unawareness, and acceptance produces the opposite effect in J. It is almost as if the deathbed statement prolongs itself to include another level of paradox: if you don't kill me, you'll kill me, but either way, I will fight for my life, making sure you don't kill me. Hill interprets the abundance of paradox in this scene as such: "Paradox here is no simple figure of style; it has its source in the realization—already announced in Blanchot's title—that death knows no opposite. Or rather, that death, to the extent that it necessarily implies the possibility of life, is always already its own opposite, both conclusion and interruption, sentence and stay of execution."[97] This understanding of opposition in Blanchot—mutually contaminative rather than mutually exclusive—can guide a reading of the text, as Hill suggests when referring back to the title. The apparent boundaries that define two distinct things—death and life, the first part of the *récit* and the second, J. and Nathalie, condemnation and suspension of death—reveal themselves as evocatively penetrable.

Returning to the parallel between J. and Kafka, the deathbed paradox suggests, by way of the relationship between writing and death, that writing also functions through paradox. When Orpheus descends towards Eurydice, he confronts the issue that both looking back and continuing the descent will result in the disappearance of Eurydice: if I look back, I will lose your nocturnal form forever, but if I continue to descend, I will lose you as your possibility in daylight. Blanchot presents continual imagery that suggests the identification of J. and Orpheus—at least, before her first death. The narrator describes J.'s relationship with dying, when he writes, "In her nightly terror, she wasn't superstitious at all; she faced a very great danger, one that was nameless and formless, altogether indeterminate and when she was alone she faced it all alone, without recourse to any tricks or charms" (138). J. approaches the infinite, formless space of death, but refuses to cede her power as she returns to life and daylight. The narrator's language suggests that this process repeats itself, that J. faces the "nightly terror" throughout her sickness. In a sense, the cyclical (almost) dying and (almost) resurrecting mirrors the process of the writer, who submerges himself or herself in the approach of the work, only eventually to come up for air in order *not* to disappear. Another paradox arises: if I die, I'll die forever, and if I live, I'll betray the infinite, formless, essential death. The Orphic writer seeks death in order to grasp it, when this grasping only affirms the space that leaves death at an infinite distance. J. takes part, even if unwillingly, in that process; her body reflects the arduous repetition of her nocturnal journey, as her eyes bulge from their sockets and her voice melts into fits of coughing that prevent her from conversing with the narrator.

J.'s last attempt to contact the narrator before her death involves a letter she dictates to a friend in which she describes herself as "almost well" and advises the narrator, "don't worry about me" (142). The narrator infers that J.'s message means the opposite of what it says—perhaps that is all she can do—and that "she was announcing that she was going to die" (142). As J.'s letter reveals the intention to cut off communication, the narrator decides finally to return to Paris to see her. In the middle of the night, J.'s sister calls the narrator to tell him that J. is dying, and he goes to the apartment believing that the dying has begun. Yet, the narrator later realizes his error in thinking that J.'s sister called to announce the beginning of a process, rather than the end. He explains:

What Louise said to me when she telephoned—"She is dying"—was true, was the kind of truth you perceive in a flash, she would die, she was almost dead, the wait had not begun at that moment; at that moment it had come to an end; or rather the last wait had gone on nearly the duration of the telephone call: at the beginning she was alive and lucid, watching all of Louise's movements; then still alive, but already sightless and without a sign of acceptance when Louise said, "She is dying";

and the receiver had hardly been hung up when her pulse, the nurse said, scattered like sand. (143)

The narrator compares J.'s dying to waiting, as both imply a process of deferral that has always not yet begun and only fulfills itself when it ceases to go on. Clearly, the narrator can only perceive this truth in "a flash," if he can perceive it at all. J.'s dying therefore becomes the moment of the phone call, the moment when her sister announces the dying, as if the elocution of the statement perfectly coincides with the dying itself. Louise's statement strangely appears to release J. from her wait for the end, which is especially interesting when compared to J.'s inability to announce, and thus enact, her own death. Here we have another "death sentence;" Louise's pronouncement comes into being as it extinguishes J.'s life. That calls to mind Blanchot's discussion of language in "Literature and the Right to Death." Unlike the doctor's previous death sentences, Louise's statement does not take the form of a prediction of what *will* take place, nor does it seem to refer to a process that has been or is continuing to take place over an indefinite period of time. Louise's language negates what it names, and therefore does not belong to the waiting, the deferral, of the dying process.

While speech appears to send J. to her death, it also transports her back to life. When the narrator eventually arrives to J.'s deathbed, his resurrecting call indeed seems to bring J. forth, as if it had the power to do so. The narrator describes that moment: "I leaned over her, I called to her by her first name; and immediately—I can say there wasn't a second's interval—a sort of breath came out of her compressed mouth, a sigh which little by little became a light, weak cry; almost at the same time—I'm sure of this—her arms moved, tried to rise" (144). By focusing on the immediacy of J.'s exhalation in relation to his call, the narrator suggests that her resurrection does not respond to his call in the manner of an exchange, but arises out of it. Like Jesus's *Lazare veni foras*, the call itself resurrects, brings the person out from behind the tombstone that hides his or her corpse. The narrator never explains what inspires him to call J.'s name, but he leans over her, and he calls *to* her, as if not really believing her to be beyond his grasp. He continues:

> At that moment, her eyelids were still completely shut. But a second afterwards, perhaps two, they opened abruptly and they opened to reveal something terrible which I will not talk about, the most terrible look which a living being can receive, and I think that if I had shuddered at that instant, and if I had been afraid, everything would have been lost, but my tenderness was so great that I didn't even think about the strangeness of what was happening, which certainly seemed to me altogether natural because of that infinite movement which drew me towards her, and I took her in my arms, while her arms clasped me, and not only was she completely alive from that moment on, but perfectly natural, gay and almost completely recovered. (144)

For an instant, it seems that the narrator gazes at J.'s body and perceives her formlessness, her lifelessness, her total disappearance, and is pulled towards that terrifying abyss by an "infinite movement." One might note that the narrator's language still has him "descending" at that point—or being drawn towards her, rather than the other way around. That relation changes in an instant: the narrator grasps J.'s body, and she is "completely alive from that moment on." While much of the language of this scene casts the narrator as an Orphic figure, he appears, at least for now, to emerge as Christ-like instead, resurrecting the dead woman from the darkness, rather than losing her to it.

Turning briefly to *The Space of Literature*, Blanchot evokes the story of Jesus's resurrection of Lazarus alongside the Orphic myth. While the two stories resemble one another, they obviously have very different conclusions. Unlike Orpheus, who descends into the night to retrieve Eurydice and ultimately loses her, Jesus calls out from the light of day, and Lazarus emerges into that light—cleanly bandaged, of living flesh. But, Blanchot describes, the resurrected Lazarus only marks the blockage of a "ruder stone, better sealed, a crushing weight, an immense avalanche that causes earth and sky to shudder" (195). The resurrection of Lazarus constitutes an act of power that brings his body into the terms of daylight and understanding; his death, due to the miracle of calling him forth from the incomprehensible night, remains hidden behind the stone. From that perspective, both Jesus and Orpheus lose the dead Lazarus and Eurydice, respectively—even if the former appears to walk around in the daylight. As discussed in the first chapter of this study, Blanchot generally employs the story of Lazarus's resurrection as a means of discussing the way that reading attempts to bring the work, by means of the book, into the realm of understanding. Returning to *L'arrêt de mort*, the calling forth, the "come," that brings Lazarus from behind the tombstone resonates throughout the *récit* as a means of resurrecting certain characters from the darkness. The narrator's resurrection of J. clearly evokes the story of Lazarus, and it also illuminates his interactions with J. after she has re-emerged into the light of day.

After a brief moment where J. appears to perceive that the

narrator "had seen and taken by surprise something [he] shouldn't have seen," the narrator notes that "she relaxed and became absolutely human and real again" (145). Despite the narrator's insistence that J. remains "perfectly natural," "human," and "real," he also remarks her surprisingly cheerful mood, her healthy behavior, and her uncommon appetite. In other words, J. seems to become so "perfectly natural" that it is no longer natural, or perhaps, is beyond natural. If we apply the story of Lazarus to J.'s resurrection, it becomes evident that J. arises from death cleanly bandaged, without any apparent trace of her death. Her body, her gaiety, and her health betray her experience of death to the point that she exceeds her prior state of liveliness. The narrator observes her in this resurrected state, dazzled by her beauty and her joy. Like Lazarus, J. lives a second time as if death never touched her, as if the call of the narrator allowed her to triumph over death to the extent that she never approached it in the first place. In retrospect, the narrator acknowledges the strangeness of the circumstances, but explains that, at the time, he could only focus on the overwhelming strength of his feelings for J.: "It is simply that in those moments I loved her totally, and nothing else mattered" (145). That admission from the narrator perhaps strikes the reader as equally strange when compared with J.'s resurrected state; for a man who remained at a geographical and emotional distance from J. during the height of her illness, he seems remarkably invested in her, and in loving her, at this time. He no longer attempts to stay away, to maintain the distance that preserves her descent towards darkness—perhaps because she has now ascended to the light of day. Regardless, she appears to attract the narrator by her excessiveness, by her "beyondness"; she no longer represents a woman fighting against the limits imposed by life, but, rather, has completely surpassed those limits. The narrator prefers not to think about such things, though; he describes himself as "not giving one distinct thought during that whole day, to the event which had allowed J. to talk to [him] and laugh with [him] again" (145). While the narrator uncharacteristically delights in J.'s presence, whether he admits it or not, he only has a Lazarus-like figure to love; perhaps not thinking about it allows him temporarily to avoid confronting the "ruder stone, better sealed" hiding J.'s death. What draws him to J.—what has always drawn him—would seem to lie even further beyond his grasp now that she has ascended to the light of day, betraying her disappearance into darkness.

J. spends the course of a day living as if she were never ill, but, as it gets later, the narrator begins to realize that J. is slipping into a repetition of the events from the previous evening when she died for the first time. He writes, "I told myself that what had happened the night before, from which I had been excluded, was beginning all over again, and that J., drawn by some terrifying but perhaps also alluring and tempting thing, was reverting to those last minutes when the long wait for me had been too much for her. I think that was true" (148). The significant difference between J.'s first and second death concerns the narrator's presence. He notes his own exclusion from the first death, which explains why he lashed out at the doctor when realizing that J. had already died when he arrived. The narrator puts emphasis on witnessing J.'s final approach to death, and moreover, sees himself as playing a role. J. no longer resembles the miraculous Lazarus, full of life and in defiance of death; rather, she has returned not only to her state of the previous evening, but also to her state throughout her deathly illness. J. is on the verge of disappearing again, and the narrator will now experience that disappearance and a different kind of exclusion from it. The repetition of J.'s deathbed scene emphasizes the circular relation of death and resurrection, as if each cycle depends on the last and provokes the next—much as Eurydice must disappear in order for Orpheus to start his journey towards her. The repetition of J.'s death also evokes the performative aspect of her second death—as if she were replaying the same scene for the benefit of a new audience. In the second death, though, the narrator administers the fatal injection, ultimately causing her infinite and final recession towards death. He pursues J. into the darkness as she approaches death, passively observing from the outside as she recedes into the distance. Finally, though, he puts an end to it; the narrator injects J. with a lethal dose of narcotics, and she dies. Her pulse "scatters like sand," just as it did for her first death, emphasizing the lack of a definitive moment, or a final breath (151). Maybe, if patience allowed, the narrator could have held out, continuing his infinite descent towards the dying J. But he takes action, this time sending J. to her death rather than calling her forth. While the narrator loses J. to death at that moment, we have the sense that the loss remains an essential part of his relation to her and of his account of the events of her death(s). Following his description of J.'s final moment, he writes, "One thing must be understood: I have said nothing extraordinary or even surprising. What is extraordinary begins at the moment I stop. But I am no longer able to speak of it" (151). Injecting J., looking back as he loses her forever, provides for the possibility of narrative—a narrative that apparently begins once it ends, that speaks once it has finished speaking. The narrator's call, his narrative, his song that opens the depths, depends on J.'s death at the same time that it resurrects her only to die again; and, yet, it still waits to begin, unable to do so.

The *récit* stops here, as a space in the written narrative announces an end point. Yet that space, rather than serving as a final breath, suspends the continuation of the narrative—or maybe the resurrection, or the starting over, or the living on beyond the life of the narrative. As Derrida insists in his essay on *L'arrêt de mort*:

> Within this framework, the strange construction of the double narrative is held together at an invisible hinge, a double inner edge [*bord*] (the space between the last sentence of the first *récit* and the first of the second). There is no absolute guarantee of the unity of the two *récits*, and even less continuity from one to the other, or even that the narrator who says "I" in each is the same. [. . .] This undecidedness is never resolved.[98]

That space in the text remains unreadable, to the extent that the reader cannot *decide* what it represents. We would appear to have the same narrator, and the insistence upon specific dates and times in the two parts of *L'arrêt de mort* seduces the reader into weaving subtle references to events and characters together, constructing a sort of timeline that makes linear sense out the two seemingly disparate narratives. Vague references to poisoning attempts, to relationships with a doctor who continually gives his patients an arbitrary amount of time to live, to repeated intrusions into tomb-like spaces, do indeed connect J., Nathalie, and the narrator—and even other, less prominent, characters in the text, like Colette and Simone. Yet, in spite of the clever interweaving of characters and scenes, the space that separates one narrative from the other creates an irrecoverable gap. At the end of the first section of *L'arrêt de mort*, the narrator puts down his pen, so to speak, and announces that the extraordinary begins at the moment his written account stops. While the space at first appears to interrupt the first and second parts of the same text, further reflection upon the narrator's comment suggests that it is perhaps more accurate to say that the writing interrupts the extraordinary space, reached perhaps by way of writing but exceeding the possibility of writing. Yet there remains a demand for narrative. The Orphic writer returns to the space that is already both open and closed; he goes back, hoping to find completion in the work he reprises over and over again. He starts over as if he never began in the first place, and for this reason, the narrative is not so much a continuation, as it is a retelling of the same journey, regardless of the different form it takes. The *récit* begins anew at the same time that it merely repeats what has already been told, arising out of the excessive space that precedes it.

One of the main differences between the two narrative pieces of *L'arrêt de mort* concerns the manner in which the narrator presents his account.[99] While the first section focuses on his repeated, failed attempts to tell of his past experience, the second section begins, "The truth will be told, everything of importance that happened will be told. But not everything has yet happened" (152). This last line announces a new relationship between the narrative and what it tells; if "not everything has yet happened," then the narrator narrates in advance of what he seems to foresee, or, perhaps, will cause by the narrative itself. Rather than telling what happened (which, I would add, remains an impossible task in the first section of the *récit*), the narrative tells what will happen, or what happens by way of the telling itself. Derrida explains it thus:

> The coming of the thing, of *la chose*, its event or advent, will be also the coming of the thing to the *récit*, subsequent to the

narration, at least to its beginning, and will thus be a *récit*-effect. Thus the *récit* will be the cause—as well as *causa, chose* [thing, mere tool]—of what it seems to recount. The *récit* as the cause and not as the relating of an event: this is the strange truth that is announced.[100]

Derrida's analysis shows the strange relationship of the *récit* and the event—the *récit* causes something to open up that allows for the event it tells. Derrida plays with the notion of cause and effect as it relates to narrative, subverting the common idea that a narrative comes after and as a result of the event it recounts. Turning to Blanchot's discussion of the *récit* in "The Song of the Sirens" helps to develop that particular line of thinking when considering the *récit* as event:

> Yet the nature of narrative is in no way foretold, when one sees in it the true account of an exceptional event, which took place and which one could try to report. Narrative is not the relating of an event but this event itself, the approach of this event, the place where it is called on to unfold, an event still to come, by the magnetic power of which the narrative itself can hope to come true. (*BC* 6)

Blanchot sees narrative in terms of an approach, which calls us back to the Orphic myth. The narrative approach finds fulfillment in an event it will never reach because it has not yet happened and in fact depends upon the narrative to happen. In this way, the event of narrative remains essentially event-less; the *récit* is the event of striving towards the event that makes it possible but always lies infinitely beyond its reach.[101] The circularity here speaks for itself and recalls the event of Orpheus's approach towards an impossible encounter that inspires the approach and simultaneously lies beyond it. The narrator of *L'arrêt de mort* tells of an approach as well—whether the reader chooses to see this approach in terms of the narrator's distanced relation with the dying J., or in the strangeness of his interactions with the ghostly Nathalie, or in the genesis of a narrative that can only begin after it ends, telling repeatedly what cannot be told. These narrative-events become so utterly entangled that the reader begins to trace the continual unfolding of something that heads in the direction of an unreachable distance, at the same time that it retraces an already traveled path.

Nathalie's character supports such a reading of the text, as she certainly recalls J. in often ghostly ways, yet maintains a uniqueness that does not allow the reader to come to any simple conclusion about her relation to J. In other words, Nathalie feels like a repetition of J. in many ways, as does the story of her relationship with the narrator, but she also clearly does not completely coincide with J. After all, the narrative in the second part of *L'arrêt de mort* resists the reader's understanding of it as a linear continuation of the first part—different characters, new events, no overt references to the first section of the text. Yet Nathalie's presence has a nagging effect on the reader, and also on the narrator, as neither can dismiss her familiarity. Nathalie even explains to the narrator that "she remained convinced that [he] never knew who she was, and yet treated her not like a stranger but like someone who was all too familiar" (159). Nathalie fascinates the narrator, who regularly comments upon the vagueness and indeterminacy of her character. He writes, "I can say that by getting involved with Nathalie I was hardly getting involved with anyone: that is not meant to belittle her; on the contrary, it is the most serious thing I can say about a person" (169). Nathalie emerges as a sort of person-less person in the narrative, and her ghostly presence gives her a certain malleability. She seems to take on the form of J. and also to merge with several other female characters from the second part of the *récit*, perhaps because, as the narrator insists, she can't be pinned down or determined in any way.

Before the narrator develops the details of his experiences with Nathalie, he briefly introduces a number of other women who share characteristics with Nathalie and J. He also discusses an illness that left him in a deathly state, fighting a fever in his hotel room. The presence of these other similar women in the narrative, in addition to the way the narrator mirrors the women, suggests that all of the characters—not only Nathalie and J.—have a certain interchangeability. Furthermore, one Orphic scene after another, with different characters playing the roles of Orpheus and Eurydice, arises throughout the narrative, giving us the sense that the story is always going back to the beginning, reprising its descent into darkness. For example, early in the narrative, the narrator tells us of the time that he accidentally entered the room of his neighbor, Colette, after getting confused in a dark hallway around midnight. Despite the time and the intrusion, she strangely seems to be waiting for him, "sitting in an armchair and looking quite presentable" (155). Soon after, the narrator meets a woman on the metro who reminds him of Colette, but also explains: "I had the extraordinary impression that I had completely forgotten this woman, whom I saw almost every day, and that in order to remember her I had to seek out someone I had only glimpsed ten years before" (156). At this point we have three women who are meshing into one another and are barely identifiable—partially because only one has a name at this point and each is recognized by way of another woman. The situation becomes further complicated soon after when Nathalie makes her first unexpected intrusion into the narrator's dark room as he reclines on his bed, more or less repeating the scene where the narrator enters Colette's room. Finally, after Nathalie leaves, the narrator decides to seek out the woman he saw on the metro and enters her apartment late at night. He reflects, "When I think about the strangeness of what I was doing, I can see a reason for it: I too had opened a door, and was inexplicably entering a place where no one expected me" (161). The narrator creates his own parallel with Nathalie, using the word "too" as a means of implicit comparison, and one can even read a double meaning into the last part of his reason: "no one expected" can refer to the absence of expectation, or it can refer to the person-less quality of the woman who perhaps did expect him on some level. Regardless, the narrative, which eventually centers on the relationship of the narrator and Nathalie, begins by setting the relationship up as part of a series of recurring encounters. In doing this, the narrator begins to point us in a possible direction for reading the indeterminate relationship of Nathalie and J., and that of the two parts of the text.

Even as the narrator starts spending time with Nathalie, he generally remains at a distance from her, preferring her in a sort of absent, anonymous state. Nathalie's work in an office as a translator grounds her in the routines and tasks of daily life, but she still escapes the narrator. He explains: "I cannot say that she was only one face among many; she was less than all the others, that was her peculiar quality [. . .]" (169). While Nathalie's work seems to establish her as a laboring, identifiable person in the light of day, the narrator admits that, when comparing her to others, she still disappears into the background, exists less, is less present. This clearly draws the narrator to Nathalie, as she seems perpetually to be on the verge of withdrawing completely into the distance. One of the most striking interactions between the narrator and Nathalie comes about as they descend into a metro station and begin speaking unfamiliar languages—the narrator in Nathalie's native language, which he hardly knows, and Nathalie "in a different French from her own, more childish and talkative, as though her speech had become irresponsible, like mine, using an unknown language" (173). They both use a language that creates a sense of speaking with someone else's voice and "whose meaning flitted past"; they both experience the freedom of irresponsibility, of employing language in a playful, necessarily distanced, and almost meaningless way. But, in the end, it's not completely meaningless, and the narrator finds that the foreign language "drew from [him] things [he] never would have said, or thought, or even left unsaid in real words" (173). While the narrator insists that his playful declarations, and at least two marriage proposals, are "fictitious"— arising from the irresponsibility of speaking a language not his own—he eventually concludes: "I said too much [. . .] to her not to feel what I was saying; inwardly I committed myself to honoring these strange words" (174). The narrator seems to relish the possibilities of speaking in an unfamiliar voice, expressing feelings of closeness and desired union as if he can do so freely, escaping the responsibility of meaningfulness. At the same time, even if the narrator's words originally express something "untrue," the act of expressing those words with such abandon provokes the narrator to want to make them true. This uncharacteristically light and hardly-functional experience of language ends up becoming more profoundly meaningful, even in, and perhaps because of, its absence of meaning. In this way, the use of a foreign language intended to assure distance and strangeness has the opposite effect. The narrator admits his faulty thinking: "My mistake in this situation, the temptations of which I see most clearly, was much more the result of the distance I imagined I was maintaining from her by these completely imaginary ways of drawing close to her" (174). Significantly, following and perhaps responding to the narrator's strange interaction with Nathalie, the crowd in the metro literally carries her away, beyond the sight and grasp of the narrator. It would seem that he has come too close, even if turned away and babbling a strange language, and Nathalie disappears into the crowd.

The narrator explains that the intense encounter with Nathalie in the metro "led [him] to see her much more often, to call her again and again"; he adds that it "urged [him] to look for her at an infinite distance, and contributed so naturally to her air of absence" (175). The narrator has the desire to get closer to an increasingly disappearing Nathalie, to pursue her as she recedes beyond him. After the crowd carries Nathalie off, the narrator discovers her hiding in a locked hotel room that he rarely visits. The ensuing scene plays out much like the Orphic myth, recalling the numerous scenes where one character enters a profoundly dark space and encounters another. When the narrator enters the room, he explains:

> I had to stare at her, with all of my strength, and she stared at me, but in a strange way, as if I had been in back of myself and infinitely far back. Perhaps that went on for a very long time, even though my impression is that she had hardly found me

before I lost her. At any rate, I remained in that place for a very long time without moving, I was no longer at all afraid for myself, but for her I was extremely afraid, of alarming her, of transforming her, through fear, into a wild thing which would break in my hands. (178)

The narrator and Nathalie lock eyes, although the narrator has the sense that Nathalie looks past him, as if he is infinitely far away. He has the impression of losing her seemingly at the point of encounter, but the scene continues to unfold, perhaps despite Nathalie's absence (he never actually identifies her as Nathalie until the next morning and, rather, refers to her mostly as a "cold body" when describing the encounter). The narrator reflects upon his fear for Nathalie, which concerns the possibility of transforming her by way of his approach and his gaze. The narrator's gaze humanizes and gives life to Nathalie's "cold body" and the "dead and empty flame in her eyes" (178). But that coldness fascinates the narrator, and he finally reaches out, grasping her hand and then wrapping her in his arms. Even then, he explains, "I saw that she was mortally cold, and I drew closer and said to her: 'Come'" (179). The narrator explains that he feels that this scene has played out before, but, of course, he leaves only his perception to suggest the relation of this resurrection-like interaction with that of J. In the end, that doesn't seem to be the point—a final identification of J. and Nathalie as doubles, or some other variation of that interpretation. They remain ghostly reminders of one another—and of the narrator and the other women in the story—but the gap between them remains unbridgeable, much like the gap between the two parts of the *récit*. Rather, Nathalie and J. may be thought of as two dying women in an infinite and circular series, just as the two parts of the *récit* might function in that way.

Beginnings, ends, names, dates, and events become arbitrary from such a point of view; they simply point to the repetition that makes every story the same story, even when they don't coincide.

As the narrative comes to a close, Nathalie reveals to the narrator that she has had someone make a cast of her head and her hands—someone whose information she found in the narrator's wallet. The narrator is horrified, we are reminded of J.'s story a final time, and Nathalie seems to experience a sense of triumph, a "madness of victory" (185). Nathalie's cast, if it is indeed her own cast that she reveals to the narrator at the end, "will be alive for all eternity," preserving and announcing her absence like a tomb. The reason for Nathalie's actions and for her sense of triumph never becomes entirely clear, but the narrator speculates: "It could be that N. [. . .] wanted only to tear apart with a vigilant hand the pretenses we were living under. It may be that she was tired of seeing me persevere with a kind of faith in my role as a man of the 'world,' and that she used this story to recall me abruptly to my true condition and point out to me where my place was" (186). Nathalie points the narrator towards the darkness, away from the world where he attempts to appear and to make others appear. And so, we assume, the journey down begins again, the narrator pursuing his Eurydice as she disappears into the distance. After these final reflections on the events concerning his relation to Nathalie, the narrator concludes the *récit* by insisting again on the displacement of the truth beyond the margins of the narrative. He remarks, "But the truth is not contained in these facts. I can imagine suppressing these particular ones. But if they did not happen, others happen in their place, and answering the summons of the all powerful affirmation which is united with me, they take on the same meaning and the story is the same" (186). The narrator affirms the substitutability of the details of his narrative, suggesting that the same story could be told in a variety of ways, just as the same events could take place in a variety of ways. He refers to his writing as "answering the summons," as if he were responding to a call demanding his narrative, asking it to come forth. And he continues with a final commentary on his own process: "I gave it all my strength and it gave me all its strength, so that this strength is too great, it is incapable of being ruined by anything, and condemns us, perhaps, to immeasurable unhappiness, but if that is so, I take this unhappiness on myself and I am immeasurably glad of it and to that thought I say eternally, 'Come,' and eternally it is there" (186). The *récit* ends at a point of exhaustion—the exhaustion of all strength—and the narrator seems to welcome his powerlessness, giving himself over to the endless repetition of the descent towards the night where everything disappears and to the resurrection which marks the impossibility of the journey. As he says "Come," he re-initiates the movement that makes his narrative possible, returning it to the first words that only begin by way of this final calling forth.

Notes

Preface

¹ Roland Barthes, "The Death of the Author," in *Image-Music-Text*, trans. Stephen Heath, 142-148 (New York: Hill and Wang).

² Maurice Blanchot, *The Space of Literature*, trans. Ann Smock (Lincoln: University of Nebraska Press, 1982), 26 (hereafter cited in-text as *SL*).

³ Michel Foucault, "Maurice Blanchot: The Thought from the Outside," in *Foucault/Blanchot*, 6-70 (New York: Zone Books), 44.

⁴ Maurice Blanchot, "The Song of the Sirens," *The Blanchot Reader*, trans. Lydia Davis, 443-450 (Barrytown: Station Hill Press, 1999), 449. This essay also appears in *The Book to Come* (cited in Note 1 of Chapter 1), but I prefer Lydia Davis's translation.

⁵ Warren Motte, *Small Worlds*, (Lincoln: University of Nebraska Press, 1999), 1, emphasis in original.

⁶ Jorge Luis Borges, "Autobiographical Essay," in *The Aleph and Other Stories*, ed. and trans. Norman Thomas di Giovanni (New York: E.P. Dutton, 1970), 238.

Chapter 1: Approaching Disappearance

⁷ Maurice Blanchot, *The Book to Come*, trans. Charlotte Mandell (Stanford: Stanford University Press, 2003), 195 (hereafter cited in-text as *BC*).

⁸ For further development of Blanchot's response to Hegel's claim about the end of art, see Leslie Hill, "Fragmentary Demand," in *The Power of Contestation*, 101-120 (Baltimore: Johns Hopkins University Press, 2004). She summarizes Hegel's argument in light of its relation

to Blanchot's essay: "[Art] had lost, so to speak, its teleological mission. Art had parted company with history, truth, reality. Worldly action, science, and philosophy had taken over. For the first time in its existence, according to Hegel, art was now merely an object of aesthetic, literary critical contemplation—which is also to say that for the first time it was now properly constituted *as* itself, *as* art" (104).

[9] See Timothy Clark, "Blanchot: the Literary Space," in *Derrida, Heidegger, Blanchot*, 64-107 (Cambridge: Cambridge University Press, 1992), where he closely examines Blanchot and Bataille's engagement with Hegelian dialectic and their writings on irrecuperable negativity.

[10] In one of the final sections of *The Space of Literature*, "Characteristics of the Work of Art," Blanchot directly takes up this question of "defining" the work of art. He writes, "Clearly the work of art has characteristics of its own. To distinguish itself from other forms of the human undertaking and from activity in general is its intent. Perhaps it does no more than pretend to this distinction" (219). As we will see throughout Blanchot's examination of "literary space," he does indeed characterize the work of the art, often in opposition to human activity in the world; but he also subverts and blurs such distinctions, leaving the sense that the question of literature is always still open, and that this question perhaps remains as the only thing we can really say about literature.

[11] John Gregg, *Maurice Blanchot and the Literature of Transgression* (Princeton, Princeton University Press, 1994), 58.

[12] *Noli me legere*, or "don't read me," evokes Jesus's command to Mary Magdalene after the resurrection—"don't touch me." This reference to Jesus and his resurrection communicates with Blanchot's later use of the story of the resurrection of Lazarus in his analysis of reading. See Gregg, *Maurice Blanchot and the Literature of Transgression*, 56-57 (cited in Note 6).

[13] See Maurice Blanchot, "The Narrative Voice," in *The Infinite Conversation*, trans. Susan Hanson, 379-387 (Minneapolis: University of Minnesota Press, 1993), (*The Infinite Conversation* hereafter cited as *IC*). In this section, Blanchot explores the narrative "he" in more detail. The narrative voice arises outs of a void; it is "a neutral voice that speaks the work from out of this place without a place, where the work is silent" (385).

[14] Blanchot's interest in journaling re-emerges in his analysis of Kafka's work later in *The Space of Literature*. Rather than treating it specifically here, I will explore the question of Kafka's journaling, in light of Blanchot's notion of the writer's solitude and disappearance, in my chapter on "The Burrow."

[15] Maurice Blanchot, "Literature and the Right to Death," in *The Station Hill Blanchot Reader*, trans. Lydia Davis, 359-400 (Barrytown: Station Hill Press, 1999).

[16] Blanchot is also conversing with Georges Bataille here, specifically in regards to Bataille's discussion of Hegel and negativity in *Inner Experience*. While I will not pick up this thread for the purposes of my book, I refer the reader both to the Bataille text and to John Gregg's *The Literature of Transgression*, where he explores connections between Bataille and Blanchot and discusses the topic of irrecuperable negativity in particular.

[17] Christopher Fynsk, "Crossing the Threshold: On 'Literature and the Right to Death,'" in *Maurice Blanchot: The Demand of Writing*, ed. Carolyn Bailey Hill, 70-90 (New York: Routledge, 1996), 79.

[18] Blanchot cites Mallarmé: "Mallarmé does not want 'to include, upon the subtle paper . . . the intrinsic and dense wood of trees'" (39). This speaks to the desire to turn away from the act of categorization involved in naming and identifying things with everyday language.

[19] See Christopher Fynsk's essay, "Crossing the Threshold: On

Literature and the Right to Death," for a nuanced analysis of the question of the materiality of language (cited in Note 12). He writes, "If literature set out to find the 'real' beyond language in the form of a materiality that gives itself only in refusal, it actually found something else: the obscure reflection without reflection of the *il y a*, that affirmation that is a failure of negation to negate itself" (78). The word becomes a sort of residue in a sense; its inability to disappear, to make itself absent, always remains.

[20] Interestingly, Blanchot mentions Mallarmé's reflections on suicide in *Igitur* twice in this section, although he doesn't develop his thoughts on the play until later in *The Space of Literature*. The reference does help to clarify Blanchot's efforts to radicalize Mallarmé's thoughts on poetry's negation of everything, including itself. Mallarmé still poses the negativity of poetry as possibility, even if the moment of achievement is simultaneously the moment of destruction. This parallels Blanchot's critique of the notion of suicide as the ultimate possibility available to humans. In both cases, Blanchot tries to demonstrate the impossibility of the task—dying, the work—since the goal exceeds the realm where anything can be accomplished.

[21] John Gregg, *The Literature of Transgression*, 58 (cited in Note 6).

Chapter 2: Kafka and the Disappearance of the Writer

[22] Walter Benjamin, "Some Notes on Kafka," in *Franz Kafka*, ed. Harold Bloom, 221-235 (New York: Chelsea House Publishers, 1986), 23.

[23] Gilles Deleuze and Felix Guattari, *Kafka: Toward a Minor Literature*, trans. Dana Polan (Minneapolis: University of Minnesota Press), 3.

[24] Deleuze and Guattari position themselves against the tradition

of interpretation that tends to privilege thematic concerns while failing to engage the political elements of the text, which arise through the "machine" at work in "minor literature." See Réda Bensmaïa's Forward to Dana Polan's translation of *Kafka: Toward a Minor Literature* (cited in Note 2) for a helpful contextualization of both Benjamin's and Deleuze and Guattari's approach to Kafka's work within the tradition of Kafka criticism.

[25] Walter Benjamin, "Some Notes on Kafka," 31 (cited in Note 1).

[26] Franz Kafka, "On Parables," *Parables and Paradoxes* (New York: Schocken, 1970), 457.

[27] Theodor Adorno, "Notes on Kafka," in *Franz Kafka*, ed. Harold Bloom, 95-105 (New York: Chelsea House Publishers, 1986), 96.

[28] Franz Kafka, *Diaries*, trans. Joseph Kresh, ed. Max Brod (New York: Schocken Books, 1965), 98.

[29] My translation.

[30] I wonder if it's not also possible to read this relationship in light of Blanchot's discussion of the *récit* in *The Book to Come*, as addressed in the Introduction. If we read the text as event, as encounter, rather than solely as a telling or representation *of* an event or encounter, we can perhaps avoid an interpretation that naively assumes the ability to roll away the stone and resurrect Lazarus without profoundly betraying the work.

[31] Franz Kafka, "The Burrow," *The Complete Short Stories*, trans. Willa and Edwin Muir, ed. Nahum Glatzer, 325-359 (New York: Schocken Books, 1971), 325 (hereafter cited as "BW").

[32] Henry Sussman, *Franz Kafka: Geometrician of Metaphor* (Madison: Code Press, 1979), 149.

[33] See Chapter 1.

[34] In Jacques Derrida, "Structure, Sign, and Play in the Discourse of the Human Sciences," *Critical Theory Since 1965*, ed. Hazard Adams

and Leroy Searl, 83-94 (Tallahassee: University of Florida Press, 1986), 84, Derrida discusses the role of the center as the organizing element of a structure: "The concept of centered structure is in fact the concept of a play based on a fundamental ground, a play constituted on the basis of a fundamental immobility and a reassuring certitude, which itself is beyond the reach of play. And on the basis of this certitude anxiety can be mastered, for anxiety is invariably the result of a certain mode of being implicated in the game, of being caught by the game, of being as it were at stake in the game from the outset." Derrida's evocation of anxiety is especially applicable to "The Burrow," as we can read the narrator's evident anxiety in relation to the insecurity and vulnerability of a space within which free play is at work.

[35] Henry Sussman, *Fran Kafka: Geometrician of Metaphor* (cited in Note 11).

[36] Alwin Baum, "Parable as Paradox in Kafka's Stories," ed. Harold Bloom, 151-168 (New York: Schocken Books, 1986), 152.

[37] Laura Quinney, "More Remote than the Abyss," *Franz Kafka*, ed. Harold Bloom, ?-? (New York: Schocken Books, 1986), 228.

[38] Laura Quinney, "More Remote than the Abyss," 29 (cited in Note 16).

[39] Maurice Blanchot, *The Work of Fire*, trans. Charlotte Mandell (Stanford: Stanford University Press, 1995), 17.

Chapter 3: Lost in the Labyrinth

[40] Peter Brooks, *Reading for the Plot* (New York: Random House, 1984), 22.

[41] See John T. Irwin, *The Mystery to a Solution* (Baltimore: Johns Hopkins University Press, 1994) for a developed discussion of the detective story structure and its implications in Borges's work.

[42] Jorge Luis Borges, *Selected Non-Fictions*, trans. Esther Allen,

Suzanne Jill Levine, Elliot Weinberger, ed. Elliot Weinberger (New York: Penguin, 1999).

[43] In Ronald Christ, *The Narrow Act* (New York: New York University Press, 1969), Christ describes Borges's fascination with labyrinths and the way they represent a sort of contradiction: "the labyrinth is the opposite of metaphysical clarity, and its primary qualities are perplexity, disorder, frustration, and inevitable defeat [. . .] yet the labyrinth is also a kind of order" (171).

[44] Jorge Luis Borges, "The Garden of Forking Paths," *Collected Fictions*, trans. Andrew Hurley, 119-128 (New York: Penguin, 1998), 122 (cited hereafter as "GF").

[45] Jorge Luis Borges, "Ibn-Hakam al-Bokhari, Murdered in His Labyrinth," *Collected Fictions*, trans. Andrew Hurley, 255-262 (New York: Penguin, 1998), 256.

[46] Jorge Luis Borges, "The Two Kings and the Two Labyrinths," *Collected Fictions*, trans. Andrew Hurley, 263-264 (New York: Penguin, 1998), 263.

[47] Warren Motte, "Edmond Jabès and the Question of Literary Space," *Dalhousie French Studies* 59 (2002): 85.

[48] Ana Maria Barrenechea, *Borges the Labyrinth Maker*, ed. and trans. Robert Lima (New York: New York University Press, 1965).

[49] Interestingly, John Barth, in his influential essay "The Literature of Exhaustion," *Surfiction*, ed. Raymond Ferderman, 19-33 (Chicago: Swallow Press, 1975) calls Theseus a Borgesian hero, asserting that it is not necessary to travel all of the possibilities of the labyrinth; acknowledging them is enough. He sees a parallel between Theseus's selective navigation of the Cretan labyrinth and Borges's writing of stories about books that he imagines to exist—going straight to the commentary or review of those books rather than writing them first. In other words, one "need not rehearse the possibilities to exhaustion" (32). This is an interesting parallel, although I would still contend

that Theseus's heroic mastery of the labyrinth ultimately negates the labyrinth in order to bring it into the light of day.

[50] Paul De Man, "A Modern Master: Jorge Luis Borges," *Paul De Man: Critical Writings,1953-1978*, ed. Lindsay Waters, 123-129 (Minneapolis: University of Minnesota Press, *1989).*

[51] See Blanchot's discussion of the fragment in "Nietzsche and Fragmentary Writing," *The Infinite Conversation*, trans. Susan Hanson, 151-170 (Minneapolis: University of Minnesota Press, 1993).

[52] I would like to clarify that Yu Tsun's role as narrator takes place on both a literal and a figurative level. Obviously, Yu Tsun narrates, retrospectively, the "official" statement that Borges presents in his text. In addition, Yu Tsun represents a sort of narrator within his story, as he creates a narrative thread for Madden to follow. Madden must "read" the clues to follow the narrative path. Finally, I would also suggest that Yu Tsun's attitude concerning his future could represent that he has, in a way, written his narrative before he fulfills it. I will refer to Yu Tsun's narrative efforts in all three ways, and the reader should keep in mind that the different forms of narrating often overlap and seep into one another. For example, Yu Tsun narrates the story of the narrative he created both for himself and for Madden to follow.

[53] John T. Irwin, *The Mystery to a Solution*, 58 (cited in Note 2).

[54] Both De Man and Barth mention the importance of doubles in Borges's stories and discuss it as another aspect of Borges's fascination with mirroring. Stephen and Richard Madden could each be seen as mirror images of Yu Tsun.

[55] I distinguish *The Garden of Forking Paths* (Ts'ui Pen's novel) from "The Garden of Forking Paths" (Borges's story) throughout the rest of the chapter—often only by the use of either italics to indicate the novel or quotation marks to indicate the story.

[56] See Borges's essay "When Fiction Lives in Fiction," *Selected Non-*

Fictions, trans. Esther Allen, Suzanne Jill Levine, Elliot Weinberger, ed. Elliot Weinberger, 160-162 (New York: Penguin, 1999) where he discusses this supposed story within the *1001 Nights*.

⁵⁷ John T. Irwin, *The Mystery to a Solution*, 18 (cited in Note 2). Also see Lucien Dallenbäch, *The Mirror in the Text*, trans. Jeremy Whitely and Ellen Hughes (Chicago: University of Chicago Press, 1989). The infinite reflection is one of three initial groupings he uses to classify the *mise en abyme*.

⁵⁸ John T. Irwin, *The Mystery to a Solution*, 20 (cited in Note 2).

⁵⁹ Jorge Luis Borges, "The Aleph," *Collected Fictions*, trans. Andrew Hurley, 274-288 (New York: Penguin, 1998), 280.

⁶⁰ John Barth, "When Fiction Lives in Fiction" (cited in Note 10).

⁶¹ Jorge Luis Borges, "The Library of Babel," *Collected Fictions*, trans. Andrew Hurley, 112-118 (New York: Penguin, 1998), 115.

⁶² Ana Maria Barrenechea, *Borges the Labyrinth Maker*, 36 (cited in Note 9).

Chapter 4: The Disappearing Act of des Forêts's Bavard

⁶³ Maurice Blanchot, "La Parole Vaine," in Louis-René des Forêts's *Le bavard* (Paris: Gallimard, 1963), 171. All translations from this text are mine (hereafter cited as "PV").

⁶⁴ Louis-René des Forêts, "The Bavard," *The Children's Room*, trans. Jean Stewart (London: Calder, 1969).

⁶⁵ Fyodor Dostoyevsky, *Notes from Underground*, trans. Richard Pevear and Larissa Volokhonsky (New York: Vintage, 1994), 3.

⁶⁶ Philippe Lejeune, *Le Pacte Autobiographique* (Paris: Editions du Seuil, 1975), 14, emphasis in original. All translations from this text are mine.

⁶⁷ Fyodor Dostoyevsky, *Notes from Underground*, 3 (cited in Note 3).

⁶⁸ Near the beginning of Dostoevsky's text, the Underground Man asserts, "What can a decent man speak about with the most pleasure? Answer: himself. So then I, too, will speak about myself" (6). The *bavard* clearly counters this justification of confessional literature by proposing that he does not write for the purpose of pleasure. The end of the *bavard*'s narrative, though, certainly puts the veracity of this statement into question.

⁶⁹ Lejeune specifically addresses the topic of Leiris's fusion of autobiography and poetry (245-307, cited in Note 4). The *bavard* promises not to sacrifice honesty or truth in favor of style or aesthetics, and therefore would appear to define himself against Leiris. Again, we likely find ourselves questioning this promise further along in the narrative.

⁷⁰ Ann Smock, *What is There to Say?* (Lincoln: University of Nebraska Press, 2003), 75-76.

⁷¹ Ibid., 90.

Chapter 5: Anonymity and the Neutral in Nathalie Sarraute's ***Tropisms***

⁷² Nathalie Sarraute, *Tropisms*, trans. Maria Jolas (New York: George Braziller, 1963), 13 (cited hereafter as *TP*).

⁷³ The exception to the anonymity of the characters is found in the eighteenth tropism where we learn the name of the cook—Ada.

⁷⁴ Ann Smock, *What is There to Say?* (Lincoln: University of Nebraska Press, 2003), 115.

⁷⁵ Using the term "narrator" suggests a single, identifiable entity, which in some ways contradicts Blanchot's notion of the narrative voice. But, for the purposes of clarity, I will employ the term in a general way.

[76] Valerie Minogue, *Nathalie Sarraute and the War of Words* (Edinburgh: Edinburgh University Press, 1981), 10.

[77] I am referring to the "subterranean movements" to which Sarraute gives the name "tropism" in her forward to the text. I will develop that aspect of the text at more length later in the chapter.

[78] Linda Hutcheon, *Narcissistic Narrative* (New York: Methuen, 1984), 119.

[79] Nathalie Sarraute, *Tropismes* (Paris: Editions de Minuit, 1957), 108.

[80] Ibid., 108. Maria Jolas's translation of these phrases reads, "A cat [. . .] is seated quite erect"; "She sits there, very stiff, very dignified"; "the bell will ring for tea"; "it will soon be time to [. . .] ring the bell for tea" (*TP* 46).

[81] Nathalie Sarraute, *Tropismes* (Paris: Editions de Minuit, 1957), 63. I have chosen to leave these lines in French because it captures the repetition of the word "autour." Jolas's translation reads, "All about them was a chirping aviary" and "There was a current of excitement and bustle about them" (*TP* 38).

[82] Announced shifts in perspective would seem to parallel what Sarraute discusses in her essay on the use of dialogue in narrative, "Conversation and Sub-Conversation," *The Age of Suspicion*, trans. Maria Jolas (New York: George Braziller, 1963). Sarraute critiques heavy-handed identifications of speakers and emotions that often accompany dialogue: "'I said,' 'I cried,' and 'I replied'" (103).

[83] Valerie Minogue, *Nathalie Sarraute and the War of Words*, 12 (cited in Note 5).

[84] Jean-Paul Sartre, "Preface," in Nathalie Sarraute's *Portrait of a Man Unknown*, trans. Maria Jolas (New York: George Braziller, 1958), ix, emphasis in original.

[85] Ann Jefferson, *Nathalie Sarraute, Fiction and Theory: Questions of Difference* (Cambridge: Cambridge University Press, 2000), 27.

⁸⁶ Nathalie Sarraute, "Conversation and Sub-Conversation," *The Age of Suspicion* (cited in Note 11), 114-115.

⁸⁷ Jean-Paul Sartre, "Preface," in Nathalie Sarraute's *Portrait of a Man Unknown*, xii (cited in Note 13).

⁸⁸ Ann Jefferson, *Nathalie Sarraute, Fiction and Theory: Questions of Difference*, 34 (cited in Note 14).

⁸⁹ Ibid., 44. Jefferson additionally proposes that the fear of violent confrontation at the end of the second tropism results from the lack of boundaries between subjects.

⁹⁰ To clarify, my reading here does not conclude that *Tropisms* proposes an essentialist vision of humanity, but that the subjects seem to be powerless to differentiate themselves. Whether or not Sarraute makes essentialist claims in her discussion of human psychology in her critical work is arguable and also lies beyond the scope of this study.

Chapter 6: Into the Night: Blanchot's L'arrêt de mort

⁹¹ See Maurice Blanchot, "The Song of the Sirens," in *The Blanchot Reader*, trans. Lydia Davis, 443-450 (Barrytown: Station Hill Press, 1999).

⁹² Maurice Blanchot, "Death Sentence," *The Station Hill Blanchot Reader*, trans. Lydia Davis, 129-187 (Barrytown: Station Hill Press, 1999), 131 (cited hereafter as AM).

⁹³ J. Hillis Miller, *Versions of Pygmalion* (Cambridge: Harvard University Press, 1990), 185.

⁹⁴ Jacques Derrida, "Living On," *Deconstruction and Criticism*, 75-176 (New York: Continuum, 1988), 136.

⁹⁵ Ibid., 108, emphasis and brackets in original.

⁹⁶ Leslie Hill, *Blanchot, Klossowski, Bataille* (New York: Oxford University Press, 2001), 211.

⁹⁷ Ibid., 212.

⁹⁸ Jacques Derrida, "Living On," *Deconstruction and Criticism*, 143, emphasis and brackets in original (cited in Note 7).

⁹⁹ I will refer to the narrative voice of the first and second part of *L'arrêt de mort* as if it traverses the gap, even though, as Derrida notes, that remains problematic. I do that less as a means of identifying the narrative voice with a specific narrator—since that doesn't fit Blanchot's notion of a narrative voice that comes from the outside, beyond the limit of what can be said—and more as a means of emphasizing the way that the space separating the two sections of *L'arrêt de mort* serves both to connect and to disconnect. See the section called "The Narrative Voice" in *The Infinite Conversation* for Blanchot's discussion of that topic.

¹⁰⁰ Jacques Derrida, "Living On," *Deconstruction and Criticism*, 145, emphasis and brackets in original (cited in Note 7).

¹⁰¹ See Ann Smock's *What is There to Say?* (Lincoln: University of Nebraska, 2003) for more on the law of the *récit* in Blanchot's thought (120-23).

Bibliography

Adorno, Theodor. "Notes on Kafka." *Franz Kafka*. Ed. Harold Bloom. New York: Chelsea House Publishers, 1986. 95-105.

Barrenechea, Ana Maria. *Borges the Labyrinth Maker*. Ed. and trans. Robert Lima. New York: New York University Press, 1965.

Barth, John. "The Literature of Exhaustion." *Surfiction: Fiction Now and Tomorrow*. Ed. Raymond Federman. Chicago: Swallow Press, 1975. 19-33.

Barthes, Roland. "The Death of the Author." *Image-Music-Text*." Trans. Stephen Heath. New York: Hill and Wang, 1977. 142-148.

Baum, Alwin. "Parable as Paradox in Kafka's Stories." *Franz Kafka*. Ed. Harold Bloom. New York: Chelsea House Publishers, 1986. 151-168.

Benjamin, Walter. "Reflections on Kafka." *Franz Kafka*. Ed. Harold Bloom. New York: Chelsea House Publishers, 1986. 17-32.

Blanchot, Maurice. "Death Sentence." *The Station Hill Blanchot Reader*. Trans. Lydia Davis. Ed. George Quasha. Barrytown: Station Hill Press, 1999. 129-187.

—. *The Book to Come*. Trans. Charlotte Mandell. Stanford: Stanford University Press, 2003.

—. *The Infinite Conversation*. Trans. Susan Hanson. Minneapolis: University of Minnesota Press, 1993.

—. "Literature and the Right to Death." *The Station Hill Blanchot Reader*. Trans. Lydia Davis. Ed. George Quasha. Barrytown: Station Hill Press, 1999. 359-400.

—. "The Madness of the Day." *The Station Hill Blanchot Reader*. Trans. by Lydia Davis. Ed. George Quasha. Barrytown: Station Hill Press, 1999. 189-199.

—. "La parole vaine." In Louis-René des Forêts's *Le bavard*. Paris:

Gallimard, 1963.

—. *The Space of Literature*. Trans. Ann Smock. Lincoln: University of Nebraska Press, 1982.

—. *The Work of Fire*. Trans. Charlotte Mandell. Stanford: Stanford University Press, 1995.

Borges, Jorge Luis. "An Autobiographical Essay." *The Aleph and Other Stories*. Ed. and trans. Norman Thomas di Giovanni. New York: E.P. Dutton, 1970.

—. "The Aleph." *Collected Fictions*. Trans. Andrew Hurley. New York: Penguin, 1998. 274-288.

—. "The Garden of Forking Paths." *Collected Fictions*. Trans. Andrew Hurley. New York: Penguin, 1998. 119-128.

—. "Ibn-Hakam al-Bokhari, Murdered in His Labyrinth." *Collected Fictions*. Trans. Andrew Hurley. New York: Penguin, 1998. 255-262.

—. "The Library of Babel." *Collected Fictions*. Tr. Andrew Hurley. New York: Penguin, 1998. 112-118.

—. "Prólogo." In Franz Kafka's *La metamorfosis*. Buenos Aires: Editorial Losada, 1943.

—. *Selected Non-Fictions*. Trans. Esther Allen, Suzanne Jill Levine, and Eliot Weinberger. Ed. Eliot Weinberger. New York: Penguin Books, 1999.

—. "The Two Kings and the Two Labyrinths." *Collected Fictions*. Trans. Andrew Hurley. New York: Penguin, 1998. 263-264.

Brooks, Peter. *Reading for the Plot*. New York: Random House, 1984.

Christ, Ronald. *The Narrow Act*. New York: New York University Press, 1969.

Dällenbach, Lucien. *The Mirror in the Text*. Trans. Jeremy Whitely and Emma Hughes. Chicago: The University of Chicago Press, 1989.

Deleuze, Gilles and Felix Guattari. *Kafka: Toward a Minor*

Literature. Trans. Dana Polan. Minneapolis: University of Minnesota Press, 1986.

De Man, Paul. "A Modern Master: Jorge Luis Borges." *Critical Writings, 1953-1978*. Ed. Lindsay Waters. Minneapolis: University of Minnesota Press, 1989. 123-129.

Derrida, Jacques. "Living On." *Deconstruction and Criticism*. Trans. James Hulbert. New York: Continuum, 1988. 75-176.

—. "Structure, Sign, and Play in the Discourse of the Human Sciences." *Critical Theory Since 1965*. Ed. Hazard Adams and Leroy Searle. Tallahassee: University of Florida Press, 1986. 83-94.

Des Forêts, Louis-René. "The Bavard." *The Children's Room*. Trans. Jean Stewart. London: Calder, 1963.

Dostoyevsky, Fyodor. *Notes from Underground*. Tr. Richard Pevear and Larissa Volokhonsky. New York: Vintage, 1994.

Foucault, Michel. "Maurice Blanchot: The Thought from Outside." *Foucault / Blanchot*. Trans. Jeffrey Mehlman and Brain Massumi. New York: Zone Books, 1987. 7-60.

Fynsk, Christopher. "Crossing the Threshold: On 'Literature and the Right to Death.'" *Maurice Blanchot: The Demand of Writing*. Ed. Carolyn Bailey Hill. New York: Routledge, 1996. 70-90.

Gregg, John. *Maurice Blanchot and the Literature of Transgression*. Princeton: Princeton University Press, 1994.

Hill, Leslie. *Bataille, Klossowski, Blanchot: Writing at the Limit*. New York: Oxford University Press, 2001.

—. "Fragmentary Demand." *The Power of Contestation*. Baltimore: Johns Hopkins University Press, 2004. 101-120.

Hutcheon, Linda. *Narcissistic Narrative: The Metafictional Paradox*. New York: Methuen, 1984.

Irwin, John T. *The Mystery to a Solution: Poe, Borges, and the Analytic Detective Story*. Baltimore: Johns Hopkins University Press, 1994.

Jefferson, Ann. *Nathalie Sarraute, Fiction and Theory: Questions of Difference*. Cambridge: Cambridge University Press, 2000.

Kafka, Franz. "The Burrow." *The Complete Short Stories*. Trans. Edwin and Willa Muir. Ed. Nahum Glatzer. New York: Schocken Books, 1971. 325-359.

—. *The Diaries of Franz Kafka*. Trans. Joseph Kresh. Ed. Max Brod. New York: Schocken Books, 1965.

—. "On Parables." *The Complete Short Stories*. Trans. Edwin and Willa Muir. Ed. Nahum Glatzer. New York: Schocken Books, 1971. 457.

Lejeune, Philippe. *Le pacte autobiographique*. Paris: Éditions du Seuil, 1975.

Miller, J. Hillis. *Versions of Pygmalion*. Cambridge: Harvard University Press, 1990.

Minogue, Valerie. *Nathalie Sarraute and the War of the Words: A Study of Five Novels*. Edinburgh: Edinburgh University Press, 1981.

Motte, Warren. "Edmond Jabès and the Question of Literary Space." *Dalhousie French Studies* 59 (2002). Print.

—. *Small Worlds*. Lincoln: University of Nebraska Press, 1999.

Quinney, Laura. "More Remote Than the Abyss." *Franz Kafka*. Ed. Harold Bloom. New York: Chelsea House Publishers, 1986. 221-235.

Sarraute, Nathalie. *The Age of Suspicion: Essays on the Novel*. Trans. Maria Jolas. New York: George Braziller, 1963.

—. *Tropismes*. Paris: Éditions de Minuit, 1957.

—. *Tropisms*. Trans. Maria Jolas. New York: George Braziller, 1963.

Sartre, Jean-Paul. "Preface." In Nathalie Sarraute's *Portrait of a Man Unknown*. Trans. Maria Jolas. New York: George Braziller, 1958.

Smock, Ann. *What is There to Say?*. Lincoln: University of Nebraska Press, 2003.

Sussman, Henry. *Franz Kafka: Geometrician of Metaphor*. Madison: Code Press, 1979.

ANNE MCCONNELL is an Assistant Professor in the English Department at West Virginia State University. She completed her graduate work in Comparative Literature at the University of Colorado at Boulder in 2006, specializing in twentieth-century European and Hispanic literature and literary theory. She currently teaches world literature, literary criticism, and writing at West Virginia State University.

SELECTED DALKEY ARCHIVE TITLES

MICHAL AJVAZ, *The Golden Age.*
   The Other City.
PIERRE ALBERT-BIROT, *Grabinoulor.*
YUZ ALESHKOVSKY, *Kangaroo.*
FELIPE ALFAU, *Chromos.*
   Locos.
IVAN ÂNGELO, *The Celebration.*
   The Tower of Glass.
ANTÓNIO LOBO ANTUNES, *Knowledge of Hell.*
   The Splendor of Portugal.
ALAIN ARIAS-MISSON, *Theatre of Incest.*
JOHN ASHBERY AND JAMES SCHUYLER,
   A Nest of Ninnies.
ROBERT ASHLEY, *Perfect Lives.*
GABRIELA AVIGUR-ROTEM, *Heatwave
   and Crazy Birds.*
DJUNA BARNES, *Ladies Almanack.*
   Ryder.
JOHN BARTH, *LETTERS.*
   Sabbatical.
DONALD BARTHELME, *The King.*
   Paradise.
SVETISLAV BASARA, *Chinese Letter.*
MIQUEL BAUÇÀ, *The Siege in the Room.*
RENÉ BELLETTO, *Dying.*
MAREK BIEŃCZYK, *Transparency.*
ANDREI BITOV, *Pushkin House.*
ANDREJ BLATNIK, *You Do Understand.*
LOUIS PAUL BOON, *Chapel Road.*
   My Little War.
   Summer in Termuren.
ROGER BOYLAN, *Killoyle.*
IGNÁCIO DE LOYOLA BRANDÃO,
   Anonymous Celebrity.
   Zero.
BONNIE BREMSER, *Troia: Mexican Memoirs.*
CHRISTINE BROOKE-ROSE, *Amalgamemnon.*
BRIGID BROPHY, *In Transit.*
GERALD L. BRUNS, *Modern Poetry and
   the Idea of Language.*
GABRIELLE BURTON, *Heartbreak Hotel.*
MICHEL BUTOR, *Degrees.*
   Mobile.
G. CABRERA INFANTE, *Infante's Inferno.*
   Three Trapped Tigers.
JULIETA CAMPOS,
   The Fear of Losing Eurydice.
ANNE CARSON, *Eros the Bittersweet.*
ORLY CASTEL-BLOOM, *Dolly City.*
LOUIS-FERDINAND CÉLINE, *Castle to Castle.*
   Conversations with Professor Y.
   London Bridge.
   Normance.
   North.
   Rigadoon.
MARIE CHAIX, *The Laurels of Lake Constance.*
HUGO CHARTERIS, *The Tide Is Right.*
ERIC CHEVILLARD, *Demolishing Nisard.*
MARC CHOLODENKO, *Mordechai Schamz.*
JOSHUA COHEN, *Witz.*
EMILY HOLMES COLEMAN, *The Shutter
   of Snow.*
ROBERT COOVER, *A Night at the Movies.*
STANLEY CRAWFORD, *Log of the S.S. The
   Mrs Unguentine.*
   Some Instructions to My Wife.
RENÉ CREVEL, *Putting My Foot in It.*
RALPH CUSACK, *Cadenza.*
NICHOLAS DELBANCO, *The Count of Concord.*
   Sherbrookes.
NIGEL DENNIS, *Cards of Identity.*

PETER DIMOCK, *A Short Rhetoric for
   Leaving the Family.*
ARIEL DORFMAN, *Konfidenz.*
COLEMAN DOWELL,
   Island People.
   Too Much Flesh and Jabez.
ARKADII DRAGOMOSHCHENKO, *Dust.*
RIKKI DUCORNET, *The Complete
   Butcher's Tales.*
   The Fountains of Neptune.
   The Jade Cabinet.
   Phosphor in Dreamland.
WILLIAM EASTLAKE, *The Bamboo Bed.*
   Castle Keep.
   Lyric of the Circle Heart.
JEAN ECHENOZ, *Chopin's Move.*
STANLEY ELKIN, *A Bad Man.*
   *Criers and Kibitzers, Kibitzers
   and Criers.*
   The Dick Gibson Show.
   The Franchiser.
   The Living End.
   Mrs. Ted Bliss.
FRANÇOIS EMMANUEL, *Invitation to a
   Voyage.* •
SALVADOR ESPRIU, *Ariadne in the
   Grotesque Labyrinth.*
LESLIE A. FIEDLER, *Love and Death in
   the American Novel.*
JUAN FILLOY, *Op Oloop.*
ANDY FITCH, *Pop Poetics.*
GUSTAVE FLAUBERT, *Bouvard and Pécuchet.*
KASS FLEISHER, *Talking out of School.*
FORD MADOX FORD,
   The March of Literature.
JON FOSSE, *Aliss at the Fire.*
   Melancholy.
MAX FRISCH, *I'm Not Stiller.*
   Man in the Holocene.
CARLOS FUENTES, *Christopher Unborn.*
   Distant Relations.
   Terra Nostra.
   Where the Air Is Clear.
TAKEHIKO FUKUNAGA, *Flowers of Grass.*
WILLIAM GADDIS, *J R.*
   The Recognitions.
JANICE GALLOWAY, *Foreign Parts.*
   The Trick Is to Keep Breathing.
WILLIAM H. GASS, *Cartesian Sonata
   and Other Novellas.*
   Finding a Form.
   A Temple of Texts.
   The Tunnel.
   Willie Masters' Lonesome Wife.
GÉRARD GAVARRY, *Hoppla! 1 2 3.*
ETIENNE GILSON,
   The Arts of the Beautiful.
   Forms and Substances in the Arts.
C. S. GISCOMBE, *Giscome Road.*
   Here.
DOUGLAS GLOVER, *Bad News of the Heart.*
WITOLD GOMBROWICZ,
   A Kind of Testament.
PAULO EMÍLIO SALES GOMES, *P's Three
   Women.*
GEORGI GOSPODINOV, *Natural Novel.*
JUAN GOYTISOLO, *Count Julian.*
   Juan the Landless.
   Makbara.
   Marks of Identity.

FOR A FULL LIST OF PUBLICATIONS, VISIT:
www.dalkeyarchive.com

SELECTED DALKEY ARCHIVE TITLES

HENRY GREEN, *Back.*
Blindness.
Concluding.
Doting.
Nothing.
JACK GREEN, *Fire the Bastards!*
JIŘÍ GRUŠA, *The Questionnaire.*
MELA HARTWIG, *Am I a Redundant Human Being?*
JOHN HAWKES, *The Passion Artist.*
Whistlejacket.
ELIZABETH HEIGHWAY, ED., *Contemporary Georgian Fiction.*
ALEKSANDAR HEMON, ED., *Best European Fiction.*
AIDAN HIGGINS, *Balcony of Europe.*
Blind Man's Bluff
Bornholm Night-Ferry.
Flotsam and Jetsam.
Langrishe, Go Down.
Scenes from a Receding Past.
KEIZO HINO, *Isle of Dreams.*
KAZUSHI HOSAKA, *Plainsong.*
ALDOUS HUXLEY, *Antic Hay.*
Crome Yellow.
Point Counter Point.
Those Barren Leaves.
Time Must Have a Stop.
NAOYUKI II, *The Shadow of a Blue Cat.*
GERT JONKE, *The Distant Sound.*
Geometric Regional Novel.
Homage to Czerny.
The System of Vienna.
JACQUES JOUET, *Mountain R.*
Savage.
Upstaged.
MIEKO KANAI, *The Word Book.*
YORAM KANIUK, *Life on Sandpaper.*
HUGH KENNER, *Flaubert.*
Joyce and Beckett: The Stoic Comedians.
Joyce's Voices.
DANILO KIŠ, *The Attic.*
Garden, Ashes.
The Lute and the Scars
Psalm 44.
A Tomb for Boris Davidovich.
ANITA KONKKA, *A Fool's Paradise.*
GEORGE KONRÁD, *The City Builder.*
TADEUSZ KONWICKI, *A Minor Apocalypse.*
The Polish Complex.
MENIS KOUMANDAREAS, *Koula.*
ELAINE KRAF, *The Princess of 72nd Street.*
JIM KRUSOE, *Iceland.*
AYŞE KULIN, *Farewell: A Mansion in Occupied Istanbul.*
EMILIO LASCANO TEGUI, *On Elegance While Sleeping.*
ERIC LAURRENT, *Do Not Touch.*
VIOLETTE LEDUC, *La Bâtarde.*
EDOUARD LEVÉ, *Autoportrait.*
Suicide.
MARIO LEVI, *Istanbul Was a Fairy Tale.*
DEBORAH LEVY, *Billy and Girl.*
JOSÉ LEZAMA LIMA, *Paradiso.*
ROSA LIKSOM, *Dark Paradise.*
OSMAN LINS, *Avalovara.*
The Queen of the Prisons of Greece.
ALF MAC LOCHLAINN, *The Corpus in the Library.*
Out of Focus.
RON LOEWINSOHN, *Magnetic Field(s).*
MINA LOY, *Stories and Essays of Mina Loy.*

D. KEITH MANO, *Take Five.*
MICHELINE AHARONIAN MARCOM, *The Mirror in the Well.*
BEN MARCUS, *The Age of Wire and String.*
WALLACE MARKFIELD, *Teitlebaum's Window.*
To an Early Grave.
DAVID MARKSON, *Reader's Block.*
Wittgenstein's Mistress.
CAROLE MASO, *AVA.*
LADISLAV MATEJKA AND KRYSTYNA POMORSKA, EDS., *Readings in Russian Poetics: Formalist and Structuralist Views.*
HARRY MATHEWS, *Cigarettes.*
The Conversions.
The Human Country: New and Collected Stories.
The Journalist.
My Life in CIA.
Singular Pleasures.
The Sinking of the Odradek Stadium.
Tlooth.
JOSEPH MCELROY, *Night Soul and Other Stories.*
ABDELWAHAB MEDDEB, *Talismano.*
GERHARD MEIER, *Isle of the Dead.*
HERMAN MELVILLE, *The Confidence-Man.*
AMANDA MICHALOPOULOU, *I'd Like.*
STEVEN MILLHAUSER, *The Barnum Museum.*
In the Penny Arcade.
RALPH J. MILLS, JR., *Essays on Poetry.*
MOMUS, *The Book of Jokes.*
CHRISTINE MONTALBETTI, *The Origin of Man.*
Western.
OLIVE MOORE, *Spleen.*
NICHOLAS MOSLEY, *Accident.*
Assassins.
Catastrophe Practice.
Experience and Religion.
A Garden of Trees.
Hopeful Monsters.
Imago Bird.
Impossible Object.
Inventing God.
Judith.
Look at the Dark.
Natalie Natalia.
Serpent.
Time at War.
WARREN MOTTE, *Fables of the Novel: French Fiction since 1990.*
Fiction Now: The French Novel in the 21st Century.
Oulipo: A Primer of Potential Literature.
GERALD MURNANE, *Barley Patch.*
Inland.
YVES NAVARRE, *Our Share of Time.*
Sweet Tooth.
DOROTHY NELSON, *In Night's City.*
Tar and Feathers.
ESHKOL NEVO, *Homesick.*
WILFRIDO D. NOLLEDO, *But for the Lovers.*
FLANN O'BRIEN, *At Swim-Two-Birds.*
The Best of Myles.
The Dalkey Archive.
The Hard Life.
The Poor Mouth.

FOR A FULL LIST OF PUBLICATIONS, VISIT:
www.dalkeyarchive.com

SELECTED DALKEY ARCHIVE TITLES

The Third Policeman.
CLAUDE OLLIER, The Mise-en-Scène.
   Wert and the Life Without End.
GIOVANNI ORELLI, Walaschek's Dream.
PATRIK OUŘEDNÍK, Europeana.
   The Opportune Moment, 1855.
BORIS PAHOR, Necropolis.
FERNANDO DEL PASO, News from the Empire.
   Palinuro of Mexico.
ROBERT PINGET, The Inquisitory.
   Mahu or The Material.
   Trio.
MANUEL PUIG, Betrayed by Rita Hayworth.
   The Buenos Aires Affair.
   Heartbreak Tango.
RAYMOND QUENEAU, The Last Days.
   Odile.
   Pierrot Mon Ami.
   Saint Glinglin.
ANN QUIN, Berg.
   Passages.
   Three.
   Tripticks.
ISHMAEL REED, The Free-Lance Pallbearers.
   The Last Days of Louisiana Red.
   Ishmael Reed: The Plays.
   Juice!
   Reckless Eyeballing.
   The Terrible Threes.
   The Terrible Twos.
   Yellow Back Radio Broke-Down.
JASIA REICHARDT, 15 Journeys Warsaw
   to London.
NOËLLE REVAZ, With the Animals.
JOÃO UBALDO RIBEIRO, House of the
   Fortunate Buddhas.
JEAN RICARDOU, Place Names.
RAINER MARIA RILKE, The Notebooks of
   Malte Laurids Brigge.
JULIÁN RÍOS, The House of Ulysses.
   Larva: A Midsummer Night's Babel.
   Poundemonium.
   Procession of Shadows.
AUGUSTO ROA BASTOS, I the Supreme.
DANIËL ROBBERECHTS, Arriving in Avignon.
JEAN ROLIN, The Explosion of the
   Radiator Hose.
OLIVIER ROLIN, Hotel Crystal.
ALIX CLEO ROUBAUD, Alix's Journal.
JACQUES ROUBAUD, The Form of a
   City Changes Faster, Alas, Than
   the Human Heart.
   The Great Fire of London.
   Hortense in Exile.
   Hortense Is Abducted.
   The Loop.
   Mathematics:
   The Plurality of Worlds of Lewis.
   The Princess Hoppy.
   Some Thing Black.
RAYMOND ROUSSEL, Impressions of Africa.
VEDRANA RUDAN, Night.
STIG SÆTERBAKKEN, Siamese.
   Self Control.
LYDIE SALVAYRE, The Company of Ghosts.
   The Lecture.
   The Power of Flies.
LUIS RAFAEL SÁNCHEZ,
   Macho Camacho's Beat.
SEVERO SARDUY, Cobra & Maitreya.

NATHALIE SARRAUTE,
   Do You Hear Them?
   Martereau.
   The Planetarium.
ARNO SCHMIDT, Collected Novellas.
   Collected Stories.
   Nobodaddy's Children.
   Two Novels.
ASAF SCHURR, Motti.
GAIL SCOTT, My Paris.
DAMION SEARLS, What We Were Doing
   and Where We Were Going.
JUNE AKERS SEESE,
   Is This What Other Women Feel Too?
   What Waiting Really Means.
BERNARD SHARE, Inish.
   Transit.
VIKTOR SHKLOVSKY, Bowstring.
   Knight's Move.
   A Sentimental Journey:
   Memoirs 1917–1922.
   Energy of Delusion: A Book on Plot.
   Literature and Cinematography.
   Theory of Prose.
   Third Factory.
   Zoo, or Letters Not about Love.
PIERRE SINIAC, The Collaborators.
KJERSTI A. SKOMSVOLD, The Faster I Walk,
   the Smaller I Am.
JOSEF ŠKVORECKÝ, The Engineer of
   Human Souls.
GILBERT SORRENTINO,
   Aberration of Starlight.
   Blue Pastoral.
   Crystal Vision.
   Imaginative Qualities of Actual
   Things.
   Mulligan Stew.
   Pack of Lies.
   Red the Fiend.
   The Sky Changes.
   Something Said.
   Splendide-Hôtel.
   Steelwork.
   Under the Shadow.
W. M. SPACKMAN, The Complete Fiction.
ANDRZEJ STASIUK, Dukla.
   Fado.
GERTRUDE STEIN, The Making of Americans.
   A Novel of Thank You.
LARS SVENDSEN, A Philosophy of Evil.
PIOTR SZEWC, Annihilation.
GONÇALO M. TAVARES, Jerusalem.
   Joseph Walser's Machine.
   Learning to Pray in the Age of
   Technique.
LUCIAN DAN TEODOROVICI,
   Our Circus Presents . . .
NIKANOR TERATOLOGEN, Assisted Living.
STEFAN THEMERSON, Hobson's Island.
   The Mystery of the Sardine.
   Tom Harris.
TAEKO TOMIOKA, Building Waves.
JOHN TOOMEY, Sleepwalker.
JEAN-PHILIPPE TOUSSAINT, The Bathroom.
   Camera.
   Monsieur.
   Reticence.
   Running Away.
   Self-Portrait Abroad.
   Television.
   The Truth about Marie.

FOR A FULL LIST OF PUBLICATIONS, VISIT:
www.dalkeyarchive.com

SELECTED DALKEY ARCHIVE TITLES

DUMITRU TSEPENEAG, *Hotel Europa.*
  The Necessary Marriage.
  Pigeon Post.
  Vain Art of the Fugue.
ESTHER TUSQUETS, *Stranded.*
DUBRAVKA UGRESIC, *Lend Me Your Character.*
  Thank You for Not Reading.
TOR ULVEN, *Replacement.*
MATI UNT, *Brecht at Night.*
  Diary of a Blood Donor.
  Things in the Night.
ÁLVARO URIBE AND OLIVIA SEARS, EDS.,
  Best of Contemporary Mexican Fiction.
ELOY URROZ, *Friction.*
  The Obstacles.
LUISA VALENZUELA, *Dark Desires and the Others.*
  He Who Searches.
PAUL VERHAEGHEN, *Omega Minor.*
AGLAJA VETERANYI, *Why the Child Is Cooking in the Polenta.*
BORIS VIAN, *Heartsnatcher.*
LLORENÇ VILLALONGA, *The Dolls' Room.*
TOOMAS VINT, *An Unending Landscape.*
ORNELA VORPSI, *The Country Where No One Ever Dies.*
AUSTRYN WAINHOUSE, *Hedyphagetica.*
CURTIS WHITE, *America's Magic Mountain.*
  The Idea of Home.
  Memories of My Father Watching TV.
  Requiem.

DIANE WILLIAMS, *Excitability: Selected Stories.*
  Romancer Erector.
DOUGLAS WOOLF, *Wall to Wall.*
  Ya! & John-Juan.
JAY WRIGHT, *Polynomials and Pollen.*
  The Presentable Art of Reading Absence.
PHILIP WYLIE, *Generation of Vipers.*
MARGUERITE YOUNG, *Angel in the Forest.*
  Miss MacIntosh, My Darling.
REYOUNG, *Unbabbling.*
VLADO ŽABOT, *The Succubus.*
ZORAN ŽIVKOVIĆ, *Hidden Camera.*
LOUIS ZUKOFSKY, *Collected Fiction.*
VITOMIL ZUPAN, *Minuet for Guitar.*
SCOTT ZWIREN, *God Head.*

FOR A FULL LIST OF PUBLICATIONS, VISIT:
www.dalkeyarchive.com

www.ingramcontent.com/pod-product-compliance
Lightning Source LLC
Chambersburg PA
CBHW020407080526
44584CB00014B/1211